100 years of OZ

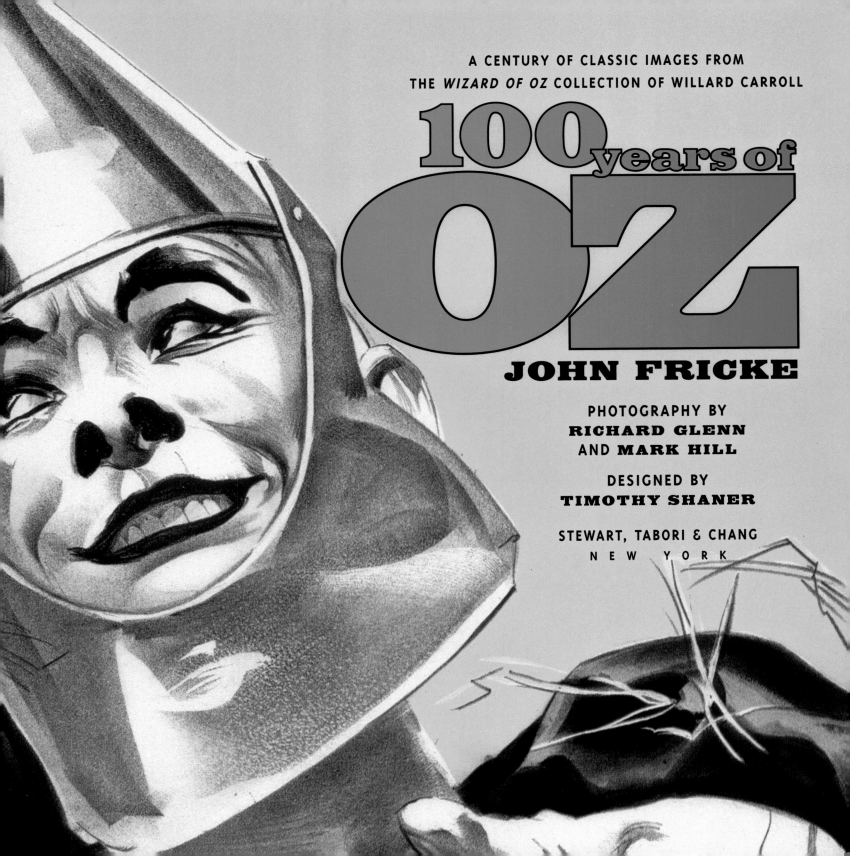

A CENTURY OF CLASSIC IMAGES FROM
THE *WIZARD OF OZ* COLLECTION OF WILLARD CARROLL

100 *years of* OZ

JOHN FRICKE

PHOTOGRAPHY BY
RICHARD GLENN
AND **MARK HILL**

DESIGNED BY
TIMOTHY SHANER

Stewart, Tabori & Chang
NEW YORK

Dedication

For my mother, Dorothy. The first and—all apologies
to Baum—the best.   —Willard Carroll

For my parents, Wally and Dottie Fricke—who encouraged
my every moment spent in Oz and who always did everything
they could to make our real world as equally magical, blessed,
and happy a land of love.   —John Fricke

Published in 1999 by
Stewart, Tabori & Chang
A division of U.S. Media Holdings, Inc.
115 West 18th Street
New York, NY 10011

Distributed in Canada by
General Publishing Company Ltd.
30 Lesmill Road
Don Mills, Ontario, Canada M3B 2T6

Library of Congress Cataloging-in-Publication Data

Fricke, John.
    100 Years of Oz : a century of classic images from The Wizard of Oz collection
of Willard Carroll / John Fricke ; photography by Richard Glenn and Mark Hill.
        p. cm.
    ISBN: 1-55670-940-4
    1. Baum, L. Frank (Lyman Frank), 1856-1919. Wizard of Oz Pictorial works.
2. Baum, L. Frank (Lyman Frank), 1856-1919—Adaptations Pictorial works.
3. Baum, L. Frank (Lyman Frank), 1856-1919—Illustrations. 4. Baum, L. Frank
(Lyman Frank), 1856-1919 Collectibles. 5. Children's stories, American Illustrations.
6. Fantasy fiction, American Illustrations. 7 Oz (Imaginary place)—Collectibles.
8. Carroll, Willard—Art collections. 9. Oz (Imaginary place) in art.   I. Title.
II. Title: One hundred years of Oz.
PS5503.A923W594 1999
813'.4—dc21   99-30777
                                          CIP

Printed in China

10 9 8 7 6 5 4 3 2 1

First Printing

Cover: Detail from the box cover of Whitman's "The Game of *The
Wizard of Oz*" (1939). *Page 1:* Detail from a set reference still for
the Munchkinland sequence of MGM's *The Wizard of Oz* (1939).
Page 2-3: Detail from a 1902 poster for *The Wizard of Oz* stage
musical, showing Fred A. Stone and David C. Montgomery as the
Scarecrow and Tin Woodman. *Contents page:* Hollow molded-
rubber Cowardly Lion squeeze toy from the A. A. Burnstein Sales
Organization (1939).

CONTENTS

Preface **6**

Introduction **9**

1900s 21
Down the Yellow Brick Road

1910s 39
The Royal Historian of Oz

1920s 49
An American Phenomenon

1930s 61
A Technicolor Show of Shows

1940s 83
Oz Around the World

1950s 95
Oz Comes Home

1960s 105
Off to See the Wizard

1970s 125
Ease On Down the Road

1980s 135
Return to Oz

1990s 147
Rainbow Road

PREFACE

Collecting isn't a choice. Either you're born a collector or you aren't.

It began innocently enough for me — seeing a movie once a year on television, reading as many of the books as I could find, and wanting to be surrounded with reminders of a story and characters that were continually comforting.

This instant childhood obsession first propelled me to seek out plastic hand puppets shrink-wrapped on a variety of soap products. I wouldn't be satisfied with a single example. I had to have a complete set. Over the years, this addiction extended to all sorts of printed matter and merchandise. Toys had to be mint-in-box or package. And, when it came to books: near-fine to fine or, best yet, mint.

Why Oz? Why this story? These characters?

For me, the attraction goes beyond the somewhat

simplistic "there's-no-place-like-home" philosophy contained in the MGM film. Even as a child, I wondered why on earth Dorothy would ever want to leave color and go back to black-and-white.

In the Baum book, of course, Dorothy actually does go to Oz and, in later volumes, settles there. When I was working at Disney at the time of *Return to Oz*, one of the executives commented that this sent a negative message — encouraging children to embrace fantasy as real was a bad thing. Personally, given a

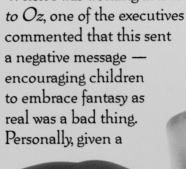

choice between reality and fantasy, I'll always go for the latter. And it's served me well.

From my perspective, the books and the movie are primarily about identity. The four main characters already have within themselves the very thing they are seeking. But it takes time and effort and the support of this small core group to realize it and bring it to the surface. The innocence and single-mindedness of a child focuses their search

and, in a short time, these four become a sort of extended family. And once they fully embrace their abilities, they take appropriate leadership positions in a community that celebrates the ultimate in creativity and diversity. After all, in Oz, flesh-and-bone creatures (both human and not-so-human) share space with men and women of tin and straw.

One hundred years after its first publication, the socially prescient nature of the story now seems even more inspired. And it's why we return to these familiar stories. They hint at the unknown promise of the future and provide solace and hope in the present.

And all the toys and games and stuff are pretty cool, too.

—Willard Carroll

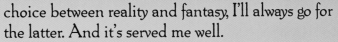

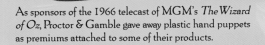

As sponsors of the 1966 telecast of MGM's *The Wizard of Oz*, Proctor & Gamble gave away plastic hand puppets as premiums attached to some of their products.

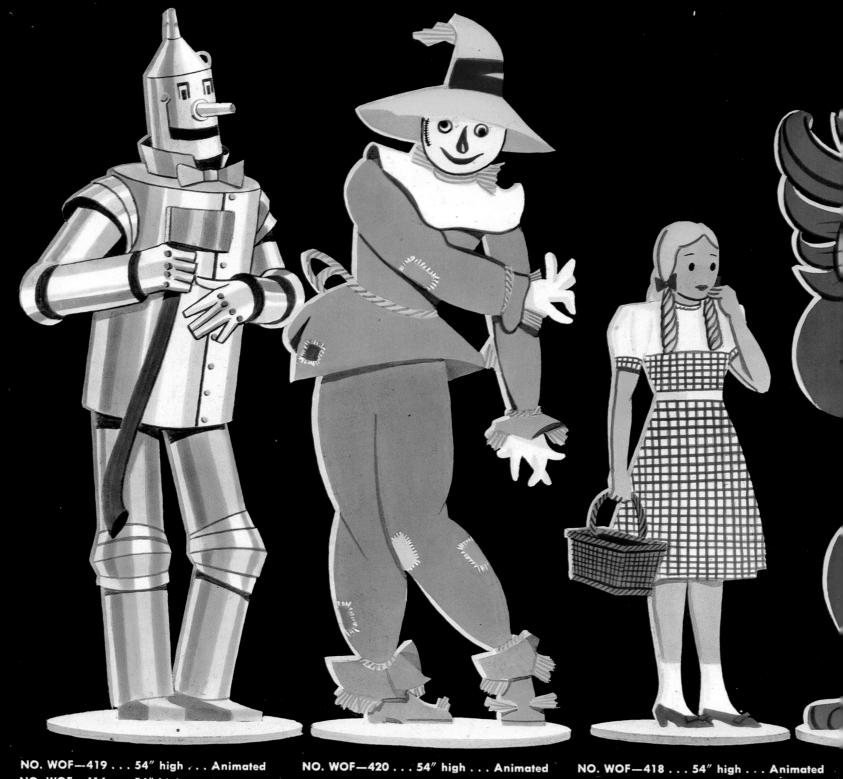

NO. WOF—419 . . . 54″ high . . . Animated   NO. WOF—420 . . . 54″ high . . . Animated   NO. WOF—418 . . . 54″ high . . . Animated

NO. WOF—414 . . . 54″ high . . . Still   NO. WOF—415 . . . 54″ high . . . Still   NO. WOF—413 . . . 54″ high . . . Still

NO. WOF—429 . . . 24″ high . . . Still   NO. WOF—430 . . . 24″ high . . . Still   NO. WOF—428 . . . 24″ high . . . Still

O. WOF—421 . . . Set of 4 (1 ea. of 4) . . . 54″ high . . . Animated   NO. WOF—416 . . . Set of 4 (1 ea. of 4) . . . 54″ high . . . Still   NO. WOF

O. WOF—431 . . . Set of 4 (1 ea. of 4, as above) . . . 24″ high . . . Still   NO. WOC—219 . . . Comura Paper Decorations . . . set of 6 figures (including

Dorothy. The Yellow Brick Road. The Scarecrow, Tin Woodman, and Cowardly Lion. The Emerald City. Toto. The Wicked Witch of the West. The Poppy Field. The Munchkins. Glinda. In the history of twentieth-century American literature and entertainment, there are no better-known or more indelible images than these.

Brought to life with the publication of *The Wonderful Wizard of Oz* in 1900, the Land of Oz, its characters, and its charisma celebrate an unprecedented fame as they approach their one-hundredth birthday. There are many factors that led to such eminence, but foremost among them are the imagination, heart, and communicative power of L. Frank Baum and his fellow Oz authors and illustrators — and the power of Metro-Goldwyn-Mayer in Hollywood's halcyon heyday. In the last ten decades, stage productions, television, and mammoth merchandising have immeasurably bolstered the audience for Oz. But Baum's talent for storytelling started it all . . . and MGM created so potent a screen version of his narrative that, by its own sixtieth anniversary in 1999, it was acknowledged as the most widely seen and quite possibly best-loved motion picture in history.

The film's fame has long obscured a greater Oz legend; the

Above: A holiday sticker issued by W. L. Stensgaard & Associates, Inc., in conjunction with the Oz window displays they mounted under license from MGM (1939).
Left: The deluxe herald for the sizes and types of Oz figures Stensgaard made available for department store use — "exclusive to one store in each city."

—417 . . . 54" high . . . Animated
—412 . . . 54" high . . . Still
—427 . . . 24" high . . . Still
t of 4 (1 ea. of 4) . . . 24" high . . . Still
Monkey) 24" figures . . on 30"x90" sheet

uninitiated may be surprised to learn that *The Wizard of Oz* (the adjective "Wonderful" was dropped from the title in 1903) was only the first of forty official Oz books published between 1900 and 1963. Baum wrote fourteen; six other writers contributed the rest. From early on, Oz was promotionally touted — and eventually critically recognized — as "America's own fairyland," an appellation much in keeping with Baum's inspirations. Dorothy Gale of Kansas remains both timeless and a quintessential Midwestern child of 1900: sunny, brave, and resourceful, combining common sense with a capacity for friendship. Her companions had their origins in elements familiar to every youngster of the day; it was an era in which scarecrows reigned over cornfields, tin containers abounded on household shelves, lions could be seen in circuses (and a cowardly beast was an oxymoron to delight a child). Baum followed the same pattern for many of the

curiosities he subsequently "discovered" in Oz — among them: Tik-Tok, a clockwork man who had to be wound like a timepiece to think, speak, and move; Jack Pumpkinhead, a carved and comic Halloween wonder; Scraps, a cotton-stuffed patchwork-quilt girl; the Woggle-Bug, a man-size, intellectually self-inflated insect; and a host of charming talking animals.

Similarly, Baum's fantasy devices aligned with or presupposed the century's industrial/mechanical age. (Tik-Tok may well have been literature's earliest robot.) Baum books referenced flying "machines" or magical instruments that anticipated radio, television, and electronic mail. He regarded magic as a science and was quick to assure his readers that the marvels wrought by sorcerers in Oz were no more miraculous than electricity and other discoveries effected by inventors in "the great outside world."

If Baum understood his approach, he did not much analyze it. At the onset of the career — years before Oz became central to his output — he stated his thesis; appropriately, it appeared in the introduction to *The Wizard.* While acknowledging that "the winged fairies of Grimm and Andersen have brought more happiness to childish hearts than all other human creations," Baum sought to move away from the "historical" European stories with their "fearsome moral to each tale. The time has come for

Above: Engraved, collapsible metal cup and its souvenir box, presented to audience members in celebration of the two hundredth New York performance of *The Wizard of Oz* stage musical at the old Majestic Theatre, July 11, 1903.

Right: Sheet music cover for a 1904 song "dedicated" to the actress who played Dorothy in the show; the song itself was not heard in the production.

a series of newer 'wonder tales'. . . . Modern education includes morality; therefore the modern child seeks only entertainment in its wonder tales." *Oz*, he noted, "was written solely to pleasure children of today. It aspires to be a modernized fairy tale, in which the wonderment and joy are retained and the heartaches and nightmares are left out."

Thus Baum was, from the beginning, writing for (but never down to) his audience, making Oz both identifiable and irresistible. And despite the prior assertion, his new American fairy tales heartily embraced a certain amount of heartache and nightmare; children revelled in it, perhaps because his wicked witches and winged monkeys were always fortuitously overcome.

The Baum Oz stories did, however, manage to eliminate most intimations of romance, a topic not as germane to his youthful readers as adventure and quest. (On the two occasions a courtship concept infiltrated his books, it originated in a musical comedy script and a motion picture

M. DeLange présente

ZIGOTO dans   LE SORCIER D'OZ

LE FILM COMIQUE LE PLUS FANTASTIQUE

scenario only later adapted for use as Oz plots.) But Ruth Plumly Thompson, Baum's successor as "Royal Historian of Oz" from 1921–1939, had no such compunction; at least six of her nineteen titles took delight in partnering princes, princesses, and lesser royalty. It was an indication that Oz had moved with the times, as contemporary movies, radio, and magazines wallowed in the romantic trenches as well.

Such variation fazed no readers. By 1960, when the Oz series was all but complete, its publishers took promotional pride when they could note that, "In a recent survey, the *New York Times* polled a group of teenagers on the books they liked best when they were young. The Oz books topped the list." The claim is not surprising; millions of volumes had by then found their way into print, and that figure has since easily doubled itself. There have been hundreds of versions of *The Wizard of Oz* alone, whether full-text, adaptation, or abridgement; all thirty-nine sequels have gone through multiple printings as well. Since 1932–1933, when the first two Baum

Above: French mini-poster for the 1925 Chadwick silent film version of *The Wizard of Oz.*

titles appeared in France, Oz has also become an increasing presence in children's literature in scores of foreign languages.

Oz books comprise the cornerstone of countless collections, but there has been limitless subsidiary merchandising as well. (Massive exploitation was not the norm in 1900; with the fame and diversification of Oz, however, Oz-as-product became a prime example of the century's ever-increasing commercialization.) The present-day competition to accumulate Oz material is especially intense as it has become an integral element in several collectible forums: Americana, fantasy, motion picture history, and as a key ingredient in the career of MGM's "Dorothy," Judy Garland. Even throwaway promotional items are now valuable to thousands of devotees.

The success of Oz also ran parallel to the development of the century's media. The fame of the first book was expanded by an outrageously popular stage play in 1902, which in turn propelled the demand for additional stories. Their fame was

enlarged by the 1939 MGM film, which received its greater glory by becoming a traditional television event beginning in 1956. Such omnipresence was further amplified when home video meant the movie could be viewed at will.

As a result, the widespread influence of Oz to date would be impossible to tabulate. The word itself has passed into common usage to denote a beautiful or unusual location. (Its emergence as the name of a security prison in a cable television series falls into the latter classification.) "Munchkin" now designates anything diminutive. The green landscape of Seattle has won it the nickname "Emerald City." Commercial products from batteries to soap to medication have utilized Oz personalities as their sales force. Situations from *The Wizard of Oz* have been parodied in magazines and television programs and adapted for computer games, cookbooks, window displays, flower and fashion shows, and anti-drug and AIDS-awareness dramas. Oz has provided concepts and characters for political

Above: Box cover for Oz notepaper issued the same year by White & Wyckoff.

cartoons dating back to William Randolph Hearst, discrediting or humorizing dozens of governmental administrations. In 1959, "Project Ozma" was established at the West Virginia National Radio Astronomy laboratory to monitor possible signals from outer space; it took its name from the benevolent princess who arrived to rule Oz after the Wizard's departure. By the 1990s, "TOTO" — or TranspOrtable Tornado Observatory — was a mainstay of the National Weather Service, designed to measure wind and air pressure in violent storms.

Allusions to the MGM film now season dozens of other movies, conspicuously *E.T.* and *Star Wars*, whose themes and images pay unquestioned homage while maintaining their own integrity. Oz references have also permeated pop songs, and an Oz-association can provide mountains of publicity — witness the stir caused when Pink Floyd's *Dark Side of the Moon* album was rumored to "fit" as an alternate soundtrack to portions of the 1939 movie. The same kind of speculation has led dark-minded individuals to conjure a visible, hanging, on-set Munchkin corpse out of what is merely an oversized,

wing- flapping bird in a sequence of the same motion picture.

Over the years, Baum and Oz have influenced (or found advocates in) authors from James Thurber, Ellery Queen, Ray Bradbury, and Harlan Ellison to Gore Vidal; even Salman Rushdie has rhapsodized about the effect the *Oz* film had on him as a child in Bombay. The greater Oz legend has also inspired new, adult-themed books, including Geoff Ryman's *Was* and Gregory Maguire's *Wicked*. Roger Baum, great-grandson of L. Frank, has carried on family tradition in several of his own Oz stories for children.

Such monumental impact has not grown unchallenged. Early- to mid-century authorities and critics complained that Oz books fell short of standard literary criteria: style, plot, characterization, and theme. But as Dr. C. Warren Hollister pointed out in 1970, the series overcame such objections on its own terms; he added a fifth criterion which the Oz books possessed to a prodigious degree — "three-dimensionality." In his words, such a hallmark afforded readers the chance to "*enter* the adventure [and] actually travel . . . into Oz."

Above and right: The first known translations of the Oz books appeared in France: *The Wizard of Oz* (1932) and *The Marvelous Land of Oz* (1933).

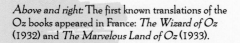

Fame, familiarity, and controversy have also engendered "interpretations" of Oz, Baum, the series, and the film. Books draw conclusions *From Confucius to Oz* and consider *The Zen of Oz*. There have been Marxist, Communist, Biblical, sexual, and spiritual "clarifications" — and fundamentalist objections. (Per the Religious Right, there can be no such thing as a *good* witch.) Essayists have addressed feminism, Freudian explications, and the matriarchy of the land. Dorothy has been psychoanalyzed in her role as an orphan; the Good and Wicked Witches of Oz have been made to represent different facets of Aunt Em or decoded as symbols of the Good and Bad Mother who "deserted" Dorothy in the first place. The Kansas girl herself is not merely surrounded by such ruling forces for good as fairy princess Ozma and beneficent sorceress Glinda but encumbered by "deficient" males who hide their humbuggery, or search for brains, heart, and courage.

The most prevalent interpretation of Baum's first *Oz* story defines it as a parable of the Populist movement, a theory first put forth as little more than casual coincidence by a high school teacher in the early 1960s. His concept, published in *American Quarterly* (Spring 1964), was almost immediately pounced upon by academicians who knew little about Baum and less about his writings; it has since been so widely circulated as to be foolishly reported and taught as fact. In truth, there's every indication that *Oz* first emerged as an installment-upon-installment, evening-after-evening, told-aloud fantasy devised by Baum to enthrall an audience of children — a reality since stressed by all surviving members of the Baum family and by Michael Patrick Hearn, premier Baum scholar/historian. (When he was recently asked to interview an averred exponent of the Populist theory, a *Chicago Sun-Times* reporter came away recollecting another college professor, Baum's Woggle-Bug, "an overeducated insect.")

Not surprisingly, there have been many more affirmative than negative assessments of the virtues of Oz; Baum's kingdom has been most realistically recognized as Utopia. In *The Georgia Review* (Fall 1960), S. J. Sackett listed the lightly incorporated lessons to be learned from the series and noted, "The[se] attitudes . . . are all positive ones, and among them you can find practically the complete roll call of the attitudes desirable to insure the continuance of democracy, of civilization, of life . . . ."

Given the enduring, cross-generational potency of Oz, however, it may be most fair to delineate its philosophies as simply as possible. On an Ozian excursion, one encounters again and again a gentle propaganda in both overt expressions of individuality and demonstrations of loyalty and courage. Its myths are lodged in the message that good triumphs over evil; this may hardly provide an all-encompassing preparation for adulthood, but it remains an ideology to be sought and supported. (It also gives children, however briefly, the carefree-dom to be children, an increasingly abandoned custom in the writing and programming often offered on their behalf.)

Finally, *The Wizard of Oz* correlates to the life journey of every individual. This may well be the primary reason the story has so successfully traveled the world, despite its many American components. Dorothy is Everychild, and children immediately

relate to her adventures. Any girl or boy can identify with the terror of being lost and the desire to return home, or — as per the film — the fear of losing a cherished pet, or the need to escape home on occasion. A teenager can parallel (whether consciously or not) the self doubts of Dorothy's companions: Am I smart? Am I brave? Am I capable of loving and being loved? Finally, an adult comes to a perception perhaps best summarized by MGM "Scarecrow" Ray Bolger: "Everyone has a brain, everyone has a heart, everyone has courage. These are the gifts given to people on earth, and if you use them properly, they lead you home. And home isn't a house or an abode, it's people — people you love and people who love you. That's a home." (Those who would degrade the "no-place-like-home" motif bypass Bolger's point: Dorothy's home was the correct one for her at that particular time. As years passed, locale and family members would vary for her and for everyone. The quest for love and "home" would not.)

But whatever the reasons for its mass

Above: The Wizard of Oz in Italian (1957) and Spanish (1940). *Right:* Book poster heralding the new 1964 editions of the Oz series.

THEY'RE BACK!

ALL THE WONDERFUL WIZARD OF OZ BOOKS

by L. Frank Baum
with the Original Illustrations
by W. W. Denslow & John R. Neill

17

Clockwise, from top left:
A Japanese and a Tokyo
Disneyland pin for *Return to Oz*
(1985); five Japanese do-it-yourself-kit character
pins (1994); four International Wizard of Oz Club pins
for the regional Quadling, Munchkin, Winkie, and Gillikin
conventions (circa 1980s); a Scarecrow medallion (circa
1920s); and an employee badge for Macy's celebration of
the MGM film's fiftieth anniversary (1989). *Center:* Two
pins for the "What Did the Woggle Bug Say?" contest (1904).

appeal, the world of Oz (whether on the printed page or on the screen) was conceived, designed, and realized as pure entertainment. And the exploration of its ten-decade history in these pages is meant as a memory book of the twentieth century, a celebratory pictorial overview of the contributions of Oz to our jubilant emotions.

Many deserve credit for all the things Oz has come to represent: authors and illustrators, publishers and entrepreneurs, Judy Garland and MGM. But Frank Baum created it — out of a blessed compassion for children, a desire to divert, and a quiet, informal mission to inspire hearts, souls, and imaginations. In a presentation copy of *Mother Goose In Prose* (1897), Baum wrote to his sister: "When I was young, I longed to write a great novel that should win me fame. Now that I am getting old, my first book is written to amuse children. For, aside from my evident inability to do anything 'great,' I have learned to regard fame as a will-o'-the-wisp which, when caught, is not worth the possession; but to please a child is a sweet and lovely thing that warms one's heart and brings its own reward . . . ."

Baum's implementation of that ideal resulted in a canon of transcendent joy. The number of lives he and his creation have gladdened and gratified may well be unsurpassed by the achievements of anyone else — if, indeed, it would even be possible to count the children and adults who have already carried Oz in their hearts, along with those destined to travel its byways into second one hundred years.

Right: Art by Dick Martin for the 1961 Oz picture books.

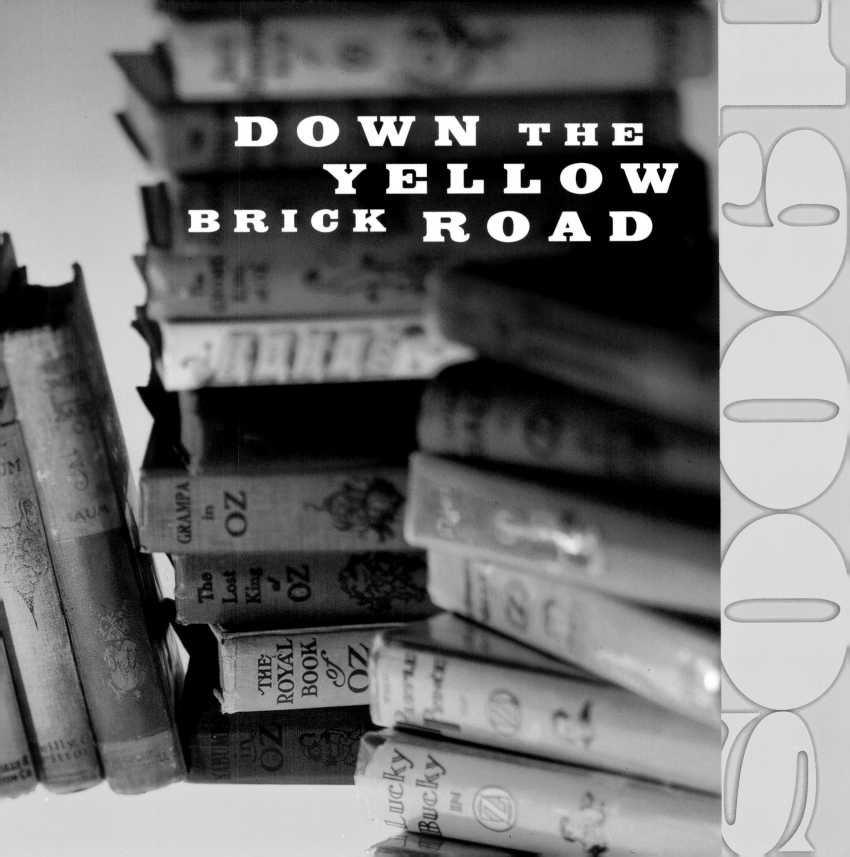

DOWN THE YELLOW BRICK ROAD

L·Frank Baum ;
68 Humbolt Park Bvd.
Chicago 🗝 🗝 🗝

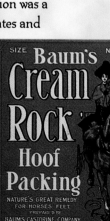

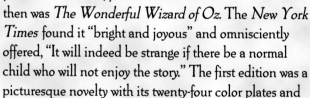

When *The Wonderful Wizard of Oz* appeared in 1900, forty-four-year-old L. Frank Baum was the veteran of a dozen careers — actor, playwright, storekeeper, newspaperman, and traveling salesman among them. Though blessed with intelligence, wit, charm, and presence, he'd achieved only sporadic financial stability. By 1897, with a family to support, he was living in Chicago as the editor of a magazine that encouraged innovative display advertising in department store windows. It was this settled existence, however — and a burgeoning association with local writers and artists — that led to the publication of his first children's book, *Mother Goose In Prose* (1897). Comprised of stories Baum had originally devised as verbal entertainment for his four sons and their friends, the volume boasted illustrations by Maxfield Parrish and ultimately proved to be more an artistic than financial triumph. But Baum had finally found a vocation; it would quickly bring him a success he'd never imagined, an imperishable fame — and lead directly to the Emerald City.

His next effort, *Father Goose: His Book* (1899), was a best-selling compilation of nonsense verse for children, prodigiously enhanced by the illustrations of W. W. Denslow. But the real miracle struck as the century turned: among the five Baum titles published in 1900, preeminent even then was *The Wonderful Wizard of Oz*. The *New York Times* found it "bright and joyous" and omnisciently offered, "It will indeed be strange if there be a normal child who will not enjoy the story." The first edition was a picturesque novelty with its twenty-four color plates and many line drawings; Denslow's conceptions of the characters and landscapes contributed immeasurably to the book's popularity.

Baum wrote five additional fantasies in the next three years, but the happy die had already, unwittingly been cast. The success of *Oz* led to its adaptation as a lavish stage extravaganza, produced in Chicago in 1902 prior to a Broadway debut the following January. New York reviews were mixed, but so potent was the power of Baum's creations

Above: Baum's letterhead, drawn by W. W. Denslow (circa 1899), and his napkin ring, engraved *Frank*. (Born Lyman Frank Baum in Chittenango, New York, on May 15, 1856, the author disliked and seldom used his first name.)

Preceding pages: L. Frank Baum and The Oz Books.

that the show became an extraordinary hit. One major manifestation of its appeal was the "blizzard of Oz" mail from children who saw the play and/or read the book; all clamored for "more about Oz" from its author. (Unlike the later MGM film treatment, the original Oz story did not present Dorothy's adventures as a dream. The virtual reality of Baum's narrative meant that a sequel was indeed imaginable.)

To answer the requests — and provide himself with the foundation for what he hoped would be another lucrative musical comedy — Baum wrote *The Marvelous Land of Oz* (1904). He and Denslow had fallen out over the division of royalties from the stage *Wizard*, so illustrations for the new title (and all of Baum's subsequent Oz books) were done by John R. Neill. A young Philadelphian, Neill possessed a sweeping flair and whimsicality that brought Oz even more vividly to life.

Baum promoted the new Oz title through a newspaper cartoon series, "Queer Visitors from the Marvelous Land of Oz" (1904-1905), and *The Woggle-Bug Book* (1905). His subsequent

1905 stage musical was also titled *The Woggle-Bug* (after a new character in *The Marvelous Land...*), but the show was a quick failure.

Nonetheless, Baum persevered; in fact, his literary output for 1905-1907 also included three full-length fantasies and fifteen short stories for children, four novels for adults, and five books for teenagers (the latter just the onset of two dozen "series" titles in all, most of them published under a variety of pseudonyms). No matter how adroit the work, however, he was beset by pleas for "more about Oz" and its Kansas protagonist.

So, Dorothy returned in *Ozma of Oz* (1907), as she did the following year — with another familiar friend — in *Dorothy and the Wizard in Oz*. *The Road to Oz*

Left: Labels for products manufactured by the Baum family in New York State in the 1880s.

Above: Cover for the songbook issued in conjunction with Baum's touring stage musical, *The Maid of Arran* (1882). He wrote the script, music, lyrics, and starred in the show.

The Wonderful Wiza

L. FRANK BAUM, AUTHOR ✤ W.W. DENSLOW, ILLUSTRATOR ✤

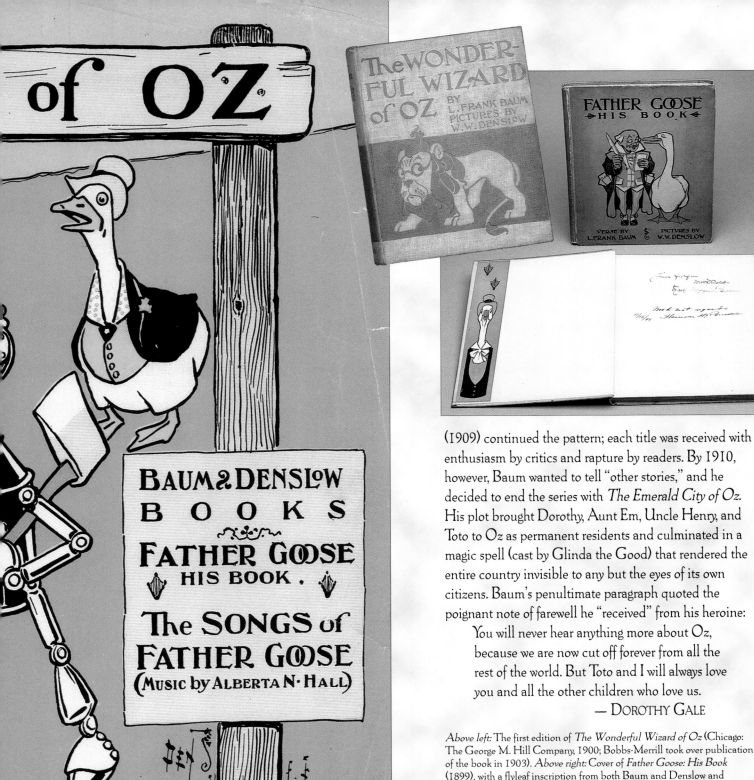

(1909) continued the pattern; each title was received with enthusiasm by critics and rapture by readers. By 1910, however, Baum wanted to tell "other stories," and he decided to end the series with *The Emerald City of Oz*. His plot brought Dorothy, Aunt Em, Uncle Henry, and Toto to Oz as permanent residents and culminated in a magic spell (cast by Glinda the Good) that rendered the entire country invisible to any but the eyes of its own citizens. Baum's penultimate paragraph quoted the poignant note of farewell he "received" from his heroine:

> You will never hear anything more about Oz, because we are now cut off forever from all the rest of the world. But Toto and I will always love you and all the other children who love us.
> — DOROTHY GALE

Above left: The first edition of *The Wonderful Wizard of Oz* (Chicago: The George M. Hill Company, 1900; Bobbs-Merrill took over publication of the book in 1903). *Above right:* Cover of *Father Goose: His Book* (1899), with a flyleaf inscription from both Baum and Denslow and friend and business associate Harrison Rountree. *Left:* Denslow book poster for the first three titles he and Baum produced together (1900).

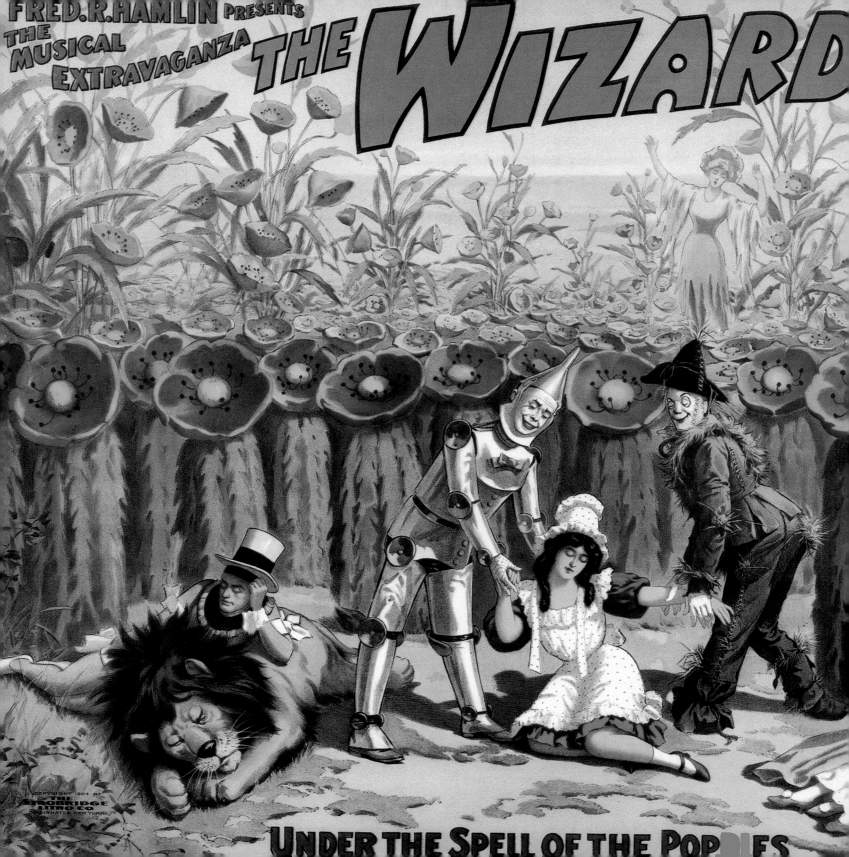

PRODUCED UNDER THE DIRECTION OF
JULIAN MITCHELL
OF OZ

An extraordinary 1904 lithographed poster for *The Wizard of Oz* stage musical. Throughout the nearly decade-long tour of the show, the Poppy Field scene was a performance highlight. Good Witch Locasta (center, near top) saved Dorothy and her friends from the poisonous flowers by invoking a blizzard; the poppies were played by shapely chorus girls. Also shown are characters new to the play: Pastoria (rightful ruler of Oz), Tryxie Tryfle (his fiancée from Kansas), and Dorothy's pet cow, Imogene. (Toto didn't appear in the stage show.)

"They now came upon more and more of the big scarlet poppies, and fewer and fewer of the other flowers; and soon they found themselves in the midst of a great meadow of poppies. . . . their odor is so powerful that anyone who breathes it falls asleep, and if the sleeper is not carried away from the scent of the flowers he sleeps on and on forever."

FRED R. HAMLIN'S MUSICAL EXTRAVAGANZA
THE WIZARD OF OZ

DAVID C. MONTGOMERY

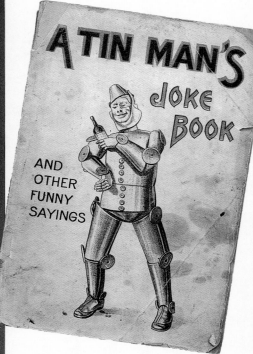

Lithographed poster (circa 1902), left, shows David C. Montgomery as the stage musical Tin Woodman. Originally slotted for a minor role in the show, Montgomery — and vaudeville partner Fred Stone, who'd been cast as the Scarecrow — ultimately insisted on his appearing as the Tin Man so they could "play together" throughout. *Above:* This paperback gag book was an unauthorized "tie-in" to the production (1904). *Below:* Self-caricature of the Scarecrow by Fred Stone, decades after he first assayed the part.

For thousands of theatergoers and more than three decades of entertainment history, Stone remained the Scarecrow of fond memory. As late as 1939, noted critic Burns Mantle regretted that the then-sixty-six-year-old Stone had not been cast to re-create his performance in the MGM film. *Right:* Lithographed poster (circa 1902). *Below:* Souvenir photograph (1903) and hand-colored postcard (1904) of Stone's Scarecrow.

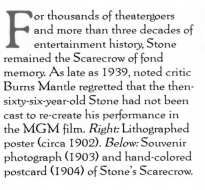

FRED R. HAMLINS MUSICAL EXTRAVAGANZA

THE WIZARD OF OZ

THE U.S. LITHOGRAPH CO.
RUSSELL-MORGAN
PRINT
CINCINNATI & NEW YORK
7006

FRED A. STONE.

The Tin Man
in a shower
of rain got
rust in every
joint. So he
must carry
an oil
can, his
elbows to
anoint.
Next
came
a Lion
cowardly,
as timid as a
bird, yet if
some danger
threatened
Dot his
mighty roar
was heard.

FROM·KANSAS·LITTLE·DOROTHY·TO·OZ·WAS·BLOWN·AWAY,
WHERE·FIRST·SHE·MET·THE·GAY·SCARECROW·THE·MAN·ALL·STUFFED·WITH·HAY.
IMOGENE·THE·SPOTTED·CALF·WAS·GLAD·TO·SEE·HIM·TOO,
AND·TRIED·AT·ONCE·TO·EAT·HIM·UP·WHICH·SCARED·HIM·THROUGH·AND·THROUGH.

Six nursery-room wallpaper panels (here and on the next two pages) offer a frieze of Denslow-drawn personalities and incidents from the *Wizard* stage musical. He depicts several comic characters added to the show for adult entertainment appeal by director Julian Mitchell, including Captain Riskit, the Lady Lunatic, and Gabriel the Poet Boy (love interest for Dorothy). Not all of them appeared in the actual production under those names (nor did a Wicked Witch or "Golinda"), which suggests that the accompanying rhymes may have been based on alternate script concepts.

THE·TIN·MAN·IN·A·SHOWER·OF·RAIN·GOT·RUST·IN·EVERY·JOINT.
SO·HE·MUST·CARRY·AN·OIL·CAN·HIS·ELBOWS·TO·ANOINT.
NEXT·CAME·A·LION·COWARDLY·AS·TIMID·AS·A·BIRD;
YET·IF·SOME·DANGER·THREATENED·DOT·HIS·MIGHTY·ROAR·WAS·HEARD.

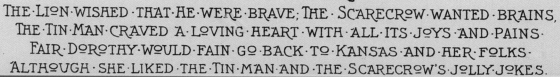

THE·LION·WISHED·THAT·HE·WERE·BRAVE; THE·SCARECROW·WANTED·BRAINS,
THE·TIN·MAN·CRAVED·A·LOVING·HEART·WITH·ALL·ITS·JOYS·AND·PAINS.
FAIR·DOROTHY·WOULD·FAIN·GO·BACK·TO·KANSAS·AND·HER·FOLKS,
ALTHOUGH·SHE·LIKED·THE·TIN·MAN·AND·THE·SCARECROW'S·JOLLY·JOKES.

SO·TO·THE·CITY·EMERALD, IN·SPITE·OF·WITCH·AND·BLIZZARD;
THIS·FUNNY·CREW·TRAMPED·MILES·AND·MILES; TO·SEE·THE·MIGHTY·WIZARD.
WHEN·THEY·GOT·THERE·THEY·FOUND·IT·FULL·OF·FUNNY·KINDS·OF·FOLK;
CAP·RISKIT: LADY·LUNATIC: THE·ARMY·WAS·A·JOKE.

THE·WICKED·WITCH·THE·MOTOR·MAN·AND·TRIXY·SWEET·AS·HONEY,
GABRIEL·THE·POET·BOY·ALL·THOUGHT·THE·SCARECROW·FUNNY·
FOR·HE·AND·DOT·AND·TIN·MAN·TOO·DANCED·ALL·A·MERRY·MEASURE·
TO·PLEASE·THE·PEOPLE·ONE·AND·ALL·AND·GIVE·THE·WIZARD·PLEASURE

'TWAS·THUS;THE·FOUR·ALL·GOT·THEIR·WISH;HIS·HEART·THE·TIN·MAN·GOT·
THE·SCARECROW·HAD·HIS·BRAINS·AND·HOME·WENT·LITTLE·DOT·
BUT'TWAS·GOLINDA;GENTLE·QUEEN,THAT·HELPED·HER·SO·I·THINK·
AND·SENT·HER·TO·HER·KANSAS·HOME·AS·QUICK·AS·YOU·COULD·WINK.

Denslow's NEW SERIES OF PICTURE BOOKS FOR CHILDREN.

G.W. Dillingham Co.
New York, Publishers.

1904

After the dissolution of his artistic partnership with Baum, Denslow illustrated and wrote other children's stories, several of which featured characters from *The Wizard of Oz*.

Left: Denslow book poster (1904).

Below left: Nine of Baum's non-Oz fantasy books for children, 1897–1906.

Right: Perhaps the greatest of these (and Baum's personal favorite) was *Queen Zixi of Ix* (1905), which was poster-advertised and serialized monthly in the *St. Nicholas* magazine before its hardcover publication.

Below: A newspaper serialization of a chapter from *The Wizard of Oz* (1909).

St. NICHOLAS
1905 FOR YOUNG FOLKS 1905

F. RICHARDSON

A Serial Story, "Queen Zixi of Ix" By L. Frank Baum, Author of "THE WIZARD OF OZ"
Superbly Illustrated in Color

If I appear as rather queer
You need not fear to stare;
Though I am quite a novel sight
I'm very well aware,
Though not a freak I'm, so to speak,
Of most unique design.
Despite my size, I'm wondrous wise
And bound to cut a shine,
And then I guess you will confess
My gorgeous dress is fine.
For I'm Mr. H. M. Wogglebug, T.E.
Yes, I'm Mr. H. M. Wogglebug, T.E.

Above: Sheet music cover and lyric excerpt
from "Mr. H. M. Wogglebug, T.E." (written by
Baum for *The Woggle-Bug* stage play, 1905).

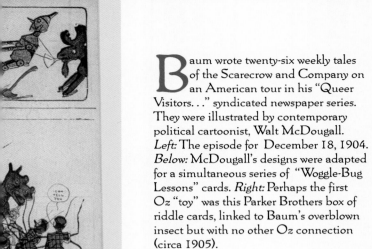

Baum wrote twenty-six weekly tales of the Scarecrow and Company on an American tour in his "Queer Visitors. . ." syndicated newspaper series. They were illustrated by contemporary political cartoonist, Walt McDougall. *Left:* The episode for December 18, 1904. *Below:* McDougall's designs were adapted for a simultaneous series of "Woggle-Bug Lessons" cards. *Right:* Perhaps the first Oz "toy" was this Parker Brothers box of riddle cards, linked to Baum's overblown insect but with no other Oz connection (circa 1905).

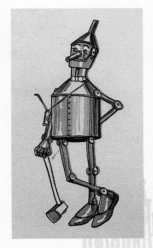

Baum with the motion picture cast of his *Fairy-Logue and Radio Plays* (1908). He produced and narrated this innovative multimedia entertainment in which Oz stories were recounted via hand-colored silent films and slides to a "live" orchestral accompaniment. The show was a critical and popular success, but Baum's lack of business acumen saw the production flounder when receipts fell short of touring expenses. (Oz came to the screen again two years later in three one-reel films from the Selig Polyscope Company.)

THE ROYAL HISTORIAN OF OZ

been elsewhere. By 1912, the author's future was in their hands: the Oz books had independently maintained their prodigious popularity, and Baum re-embraced his kingdom with happy, appreciative vigor.

Appropriately enough, the link required to reconnect with an invisible fairyland was provided by the powers of imagination he had unconsciously cultivated in his "Ozzy" readers. In *The Patchwork Girl of Oz* (the 1913 "comeback" volume), Baum explained: "One of the children inquired why we couldn't hear from . . . Dorothy by wireless telegraph." Thus, the magical barrier was pierced, communication was reestablished with the Emerald City, and the latest news from Oz could again be shared.

To help relaunch and republicize the series, Baum wrote six booklets about his most famous characters; a year later, those tales were reassembled in a single volume as *Little Wizard Stories of Oz* (1914). He also revised an earlier, unproduced musical comedy libretto, which Oliver Morosco presented with success on the West Coast and on tour as *The Tik-Tok Man of Oz* (1913).

Though the show never made it to New York, its excellent score, worthy cast, and opulent scenic effects provided a satisfactory theatrical experience for all ages.

Baum's annual Oz book was by now a happy inevitability, but he fell creatively prey to his new environment as well. The motion picture industry was growing up around him, and in 1914, he founded The Oz Film Manufacturing Company. His partners were fellow

The onset of the decade marked a fresh start for Baum. He and his wife relocated to a peaceful Los Angeles suburb called Hollywood and affectionately christened their home "Ozcot." He had plans for new musical shows, and the "other stories" he hoped to tell were launched in two superlative fantasies, *The Sea Fairies* (1911) and *Sky Island* (1912).

But reality set in quickly. The books failed to sell, and Baum was additionally burdened by a pile of old debts, many incurred on behalf of the *Radio Plays*. In 1911, he was forced to file for bankruptcy (or, as one of the more sardonic headlines put it, "L. Frank Baum Is 'Broke,' He Says"). To satisfy creditors, Baum signed over future royalties on several of his early children's fantasies, including *The Wizard of Oz*.

There was, however, a saving reality as well: the magic of Oz not only lingered but thrived. Baum had always demonstrated an unsurpassed ability to bring his characters to life. They now returned the favor by continuing to flourish, even though his attentions had

Preceding pages: A toy top and celluloid pin helped promote the new Oz book for 1915.

Above: Storyteller Baum entrances children at California's Hotel Del Coronado (circa 1909). *Left:* Sheet music for the 1913 stage musical, *The Tik-Tok Man of Oz.*

members of The Uplifters, a Los Angeles-based businessman's organization; together, they established their own studio and, within months, Baum had overseen three five-reel features based on his fantasies. But Oz Films encountered distribution problems and (once those were resolved) audience antipathy for what was dismissed as "children's entertainment." Two scripts fashioned for adults were quickly placed into production, but the company was soon thereafter dissolved.

Baum had no money in the firm, so its failure had no financial impact on him; he continued to write and enjoy life in Southern California. He often socialized with other Uplifters, annually contributing material to and performing in their informal theatricals. As an expert-if-amateur horticulturist, he won nearly two dozen cups for the prize dahlias and chrysanthemums he grew at Ozcot. Such physical activity — along with golf or a quiet walk through the neighborhood — gave Baum time to mentally evolve the plots of his new stories before committing them

to paper. Sixty years later, veteran Hollywood journalist/scenarist Adela Rogers St. Johns remembered his "extraordinary twinkle of joie de vivre" at such times: "I used to meet him taking a little soul-and-back stretching stroll down Bronson Avenue to Hollywood Boulevard . . . as he companioned no doubt with the Scarecrow and the Tin Woodman and the Cowardly Lion, and of course, Dorothy." Perhaps one of Baum's greatest delights came in meeting with his young fans; the Oz books were beginning to attract their second generation of readers.

By 1917, however, his health was failing. Plagued with a weak heart since childhood, Baum suffered angina attacks and then gall bladder and appendix trouble. Subsequent surgery left him an invalid, although he continued to write of Oz and dictate responses to letters from "his" children as long as he could.

On May 6, 1919, the "Royal Historian" died at Ozcot. According to family legend, he spoke his last semi-conscious words to his wife, drifting away after a quiet reference to the deadly desert one had to traverse to reach the Land of Oz: "Now we can cross the shifting sands . . . ."

Above: Baum's bookplate, referencing the new home he and wife Maud built in California. *Left:* Baum's *Juvenile Speaker* (1910) collected excerpts from his earlier work; *The Sea Fairies* (1911) and *Sky Island* (1912) marked his attempt to escape from Oz. By 1913, a promotional splash for *The Patchwork Girl of Oz* and the "Little Wizard Stories" proclaimed his return.

41

Scarecrow

Tin woodman

The Oz Toy Book was drawn by the inimitable Neill as a promotion for the series. (Baum, who had not been consulted about its publication, was unhappily astounded when he saw the work advertised in the 1915 Reilly & Britton catalogue.) Today, few of the fragile *Toy* books survive intact or complete. *Above:* Front cover. *Left:* Three of Neill's fifty-four cutout characters.

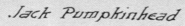
Jack Pumpkinhead

Above: The Oz Film Manufacturing Company (1914–1915). From left, Secretary Clarence Rundel, President Baum, Treasurer H. M. Waldeman, and Vice President Louis F. Gottschalk (who also scored music to accompany the silent films).

Far left: Interior of ad flyer for *The Last Egyptian,* adapted for the screen from Baum's adult novel. *Below:* Screen title card for *The Patchwork Girl of Oz* film. *Left:* The Woozy — a promotional cutout toy of a new character in the *Patchwork Girl* cast. *Above right:* Film still from *His Majesty, the Scarecrow of Oz. Right:* Front page of another ad brochure.

"Take care! It is against the Law of Oz to pluck a Six-Leaved Clover."

OZ FILMS

The Oz Film Manufacturing Company
Santa Monica Boulevard; Gower to Lodi Streets
LOS ANGELES, - - - - CALIFORNIA

NEW YORK OFFICE - - 220 WEST 42nd STREET
Frank J. Baum - - *Special Representative*

L. FRANK BAUM
Famous "Wizard of Oz" man whose books and plays have been enjoyed by millions of people

VIOLET MacMILLAN
"The Daintiest Darling of them all"

Mr. L. Frank Baum

L. Frank Baum, the president and general manager of the Oz Film Manufacturing Company of Los Angeles, is famous the world over for his quaint books and the extraordinary characters he has invented.

Mr. Baum has written and published twenty six successful books; of the number are more successful children's books than are credited to any other author. Of these, the ten Oz books have sold over four million copies during the last six years. They are translated in nearly all languages and have almost as large a sale in Great Britain and Germany as in this country.

Believing that there was a field for a new line of motion picture plays, Mr. Baum organized the Oz Film Manufacturing Company last spring. The first production was "The Patchwork Girl of Oz," a photo-extravaganza full of genuine comedy, quaint characters and pretty girls. The work is all done under Mr. Baum's personal direction and supervision and he has shown a capacity for making just as successful motion pictures as he did books and musical shows.
— *Moving Picture World*

She plays leads with the Oz Film Manufacturing Co.

Violet Macmillan first become prominent when she appeared in the leading role of "Dorothy" in the "Wizard of Oz" Company organized by Hurtig & Seamon. She was by far the most successful actress who ever essayed this part.

She was the original girl in "The Time, The Place, and The Girl," and has been identified with musical comedy for a number of years.

During the past year she was a headliner on the Orpheum circuit, when she was called "The Modern Cinderella" on account of her tiny feet and perfect figure. Miss Macmillan is full of personality and her countenance is so bright and vivacious that she instantly wins all hearts.

"THE PATCHWORK GIRL OF OZ"
An appreciation by the Rev. W. H. Jackson in the Moving Picture World of October 17, 1914

Advertisements are too often exaggerating and lead to disappointment, when the vaunted ideals are not realized. Fortunately this does not apply to the "Patchwork Girl of Oz"; if anything its merits are under rather than over-advertised, giving one that pleasure of realizing something beyond expectations. "It is better than we expected," is the best advertisement any picture can receive,

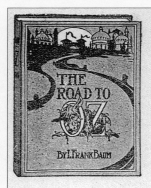

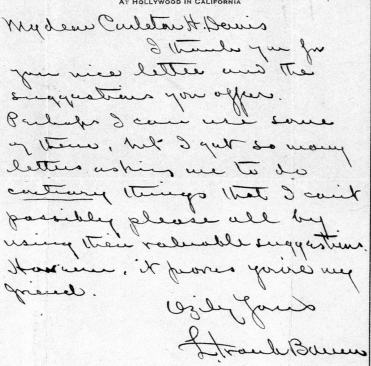

L. FRANK BAUM
"OZCOT"
AT HOLLYWOOD IN CALIFORNIA

Dec 4. 1916

My dear Carleton H. Davis

I thank you for your nice letter and the suggestions you offer. Perhaps I can use some of them, but I get so many letters asking me to do contrary things that I can't possibly please all by using their valuable suggestions. However, it proves you're my friend.

Ozzly Yours

L. Frank Baum

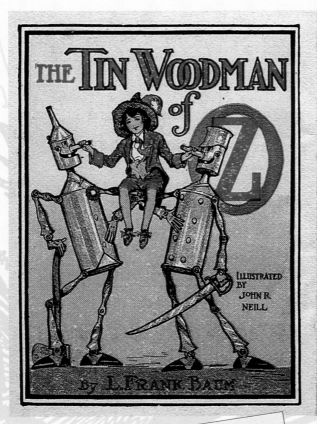

List of The Oz Books

The Land of Oz.
Ozma of Oz.
Dorothy and the Wizard in Oz.
The Road to Oz.
The Emerald City of Oz.
The Patchwork Girl of Oz.
Tik-Tok of Oz.
The Scarecrow of Oz.
Rinkitink in Oz.
The Lost Princess of Oz.
The Tin Woodman of Oz.
The Magic of Oz.
Glinda of Oz.

For Sale in

GIMBEL BROTHERS'
Land of Oz Toy Store

Fourth Floor

L. FRANK BAUM
AUTHOR OF
The Famous Oz Books

One of many letters, far left, which Baum personally wrote in response to fan mail during his tenure as Royal Historian. *Above:* Rear and front cover of an ad brochure for Baum's Oz titles (1920). *Left:* Interior of the same flyer, listing the Oz books to date. Reilly & Britton (and the ensuing Reilly & Lee) were the original publishers of all but the first book in the Oz series.

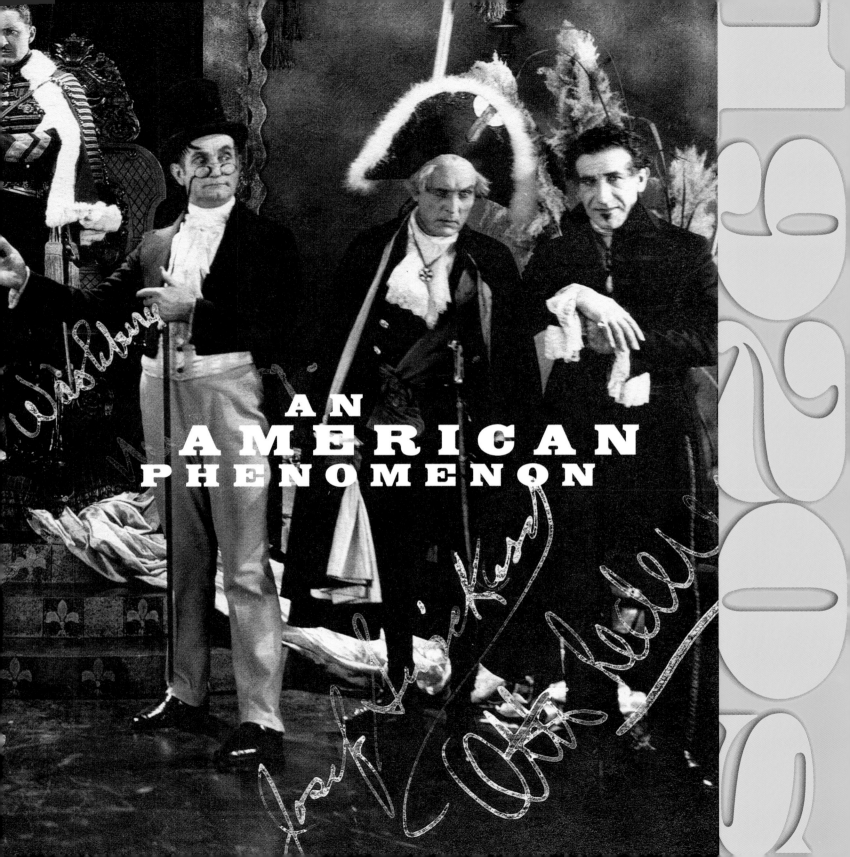

AN
AMERICAN
PHENOMENON

FRANK BAUM
10807 ROCHESTER AVENUE
LOS ANGELES. 24,. CALIFORNIA

THE "SCARECROW" & "TIN WOODMAN" FROM
THE WIZARD OF OZ

The last of L. Frank Baum's Oz titles was published posthumously in 1920; his publishers opened *Glinda of Oz* with the gentle note that "Mr. Baum … went away to take his stories to the little child souls who had lived here too long ago to read the Oz stories for themselves." But an annual Oz book had become both a staple of American youth and the Reilly & Lee catalog, so the search began for a second Royal Historian.

The heir apparent was discovered in Ruth Plumly Thompson, a blithe, endlessly imaginative, self-starting writer who'd made her reputation in contributions to *St. Nicholas* magazine and as the editor of a children's page for the *Philadelphia Public Ledger*. She was thirty when *The Royal Book of Oz* was published in 1921; though only credited with enlarging and editing an unfinished Baum manuscript, the work was entirely hers, and the transition was thus effected.

As financial mainstay of her widowed mother and invalid sister, Thompson welcomed — and genuinely revelled in — the assignment. Her writing was instantly engaging and vital, much in step with the spirited United States of the 1920s. Throughout the decade, a new Thompson Oz book for the holidays was a happy necessity in thousands of homes, and she was magnificently abetted by the artistry of John R. Neill. His illustrations in the Oz books had become a glorious "given."

Reilly & Lee's advertising forces kept pace with the times as well; their ballyhoo for Oz was more vigorous than ever before. They created wood-cut figures of the Scarecrow and Patchwork Girl as bookstore displays. Their "Scarecrow of Oz Answers Questions by Radio" was a small, magnet-and-cardboard gimmick that posed problems in Oz trivia. From 1926-1928, they revived *The Ozmapolitan*, an "Emerald City newspaper" first invented by Baum in 1904. Each edition offered quixotic gossip about Oz while promoting the latest book and other Reilly & Lee titles.

Two of the publishers' promotions were particularly effective. In 1926, they established The Ozmite Club "to get groups of children everywhere talking about Oz"; members were invited to apply for a small lapel pin and the "Club Secrets." A year earlier, Thompson herself had helped launch a series of "Oz parties" by writing

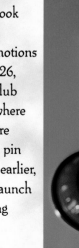

Preceding pages: Autographed still from the 1925 silent-screen version of *The Wizard of Oz*. From left: "Babe" O[liver] N. Hardy, Larry Semon, Dorothy Dwan, Bryant Washburn, Charles Murray, Josef Swickard, and Otto Lederer.

Above: Letterhead of Frank Joslyn Baum, utilizing character concepts from *The Wizard of Oz* cartoon (1933).

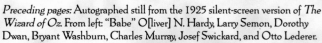

libretto and lyrics for a Reilly & Lee-promoted *A Day In Oz* playlet. The brief revue — annually revised and utilized over several seasons — was mounted by department stores across the nation. At each venue, local performers were costumed as Oz characters to herald the wonders of the newest book in the series. (Thompson also provided a script for the Jean Gros Marionettes and their *The Magical Land of Oz* touring show, beginning in 1928.)

Perhaps not surprisingly, the fans themselves were among the most passionate Oz promoters. The grown-ups who'd fallen in love with the stories twenty years earlier were now in positions of power, and they frequently carried their enthusiasm with them. In 1928, two of Baum's titles were adapted as plays for presentation by the Junior League. (Three more scripts would follow in the 1930s.) Merchandisers began to realize that a licensed tie-in with Oz meant ready consumers. As a result, Parker Brothers issued a stunning board game in 1921, and there were also Oz candies, notebooks, stationery, and party horns.

Among the most ambitious entrepreneurs was Baum's eldest son, Frank Joslyn. Overseas in the military when his father died, Frank envisioned himself as the next Royal Historian. By the time he put himself forth for the job, however, Thompson had already been selected. So

the young Baum marketed Oz in his own way, creating a set of character dolls in 1924. The next year, as "L. Frank Baum, Jr.," he cowrote a silent-screen adaptation of *The Wizard of Oz* as a showcase for comic Larry Semon. Unfortunately, the scenario wandered far from the original story: Dorothy was a young flapper and "lost" princess of Oz, which cued in a requisite 1920s romance with "Prince Kynd" of the Emerald City. The Scarecrow, Tin Woodman, Cowardly Lion, and Wizard were only tangentially involved in the manic plot, while "Prime Minister Kruel," "Ambassador Wikked," and "Lady Vishuss" sought to overthrow Dorothy's claim to the throne. The film was a fiasco.

But Oz was so magically entrenched that it survived even such a cinematic mauling. This was quietly demonstrated when the University of Washington Chapbooks published Edward Wagenknecht's *Utopia Americana* (1929). For the first time, an appreciative scholar formally appraised Baum's vision. Although Oz was (and continued to be) all about entertainment, this was its initial recognition as a unique contribution to American popular literature.

Left: Toy party horns illustrated with characters from *The Land of Oz* (circa 1920s). *Above left:* Whyte & Wyckoff notebook with an Oz book color plate as its cover (1929).

Above: Program cover for the Belgian release of the 1925 silent film *Wizard*.

51

THE
WONDERFUL
GAME of
OZ

COPYRIGHT 1921 BY
PARKER BROTHERS INC.
SALEM, MASS., NEW YORK, LONDON
Registered U.S. Patent Office

The box cover, instructions, Oz-map-board, and playing pieces for the bright and elaborate Parker Brothers game (1921). When the game was later reissued, the pewter figurines of Oz characters were replaced by wooden markers.

An Ozzy lapel pin was one of the membership benefits in Reilly & Lee's promotional Ozmite Club (1926). *Below:* Prospective Ozmites filled out this application and subsequently received *The Ozmapolitan* newspaper and the "Club Secrets." These included both "the Ozzy sign" (a hand greeting by which members could identify each other) and "the Ozzy word" for the year (the nonsense creation "Ozmickaduk").

"Oh yes; I

am anxious,"

returned the

Scarecrow.

"It is such an

uncomfortable

feeling to know

one is a fool."

A cardboard stand-up advertisement for the 1922 Oz book. Kabumpo — "the elegant elephant of Oz" — proved to be one of Ruth Plumly Thompson's most popular creations, and he figured prominently in three of her subsequent stories as well. *Left:* Oz characters decorated the cover of a Whitman's Wonderbox of children's candy (1926).

Ever the aspiring entrepreneur, Frank J. Baum developed a series of Oz dolls in 1924. Unfortunately, the attractive Fabrikoid toys were only minimally marketed; the next year, Reilly & Lee individually boxed and sold his remaining stock of the Scarecrow, Tin Woodman, Jack Pumpkinhead, and the Patchwork Girl, each with its appropriately titled Oz book.

Two additional, oversized Frank J. Baum Oz dolls from 1924. The Scarecrow on the left is the manufacturer's prototype; on the right is the marketed final product. Like Baum's smaller dolls, it was poorly distributed — a dubious honor it shared with the center Scarecrow, manufactured fifteen years later by Knickerbocker as an MGM movie tie-in.

The Patchwork Girl of OZ

Reilly & Lee liberally promoted Oz in the 1920s. The Scarecrow and Patchwork Girl figures were designed as in-store heralds for 1926 and 1927 (respectively); a cardboard sign announcing the new Oz book could be slotted in the top of either wooden stand-up. *Below center:* This magnetized trivia game was produced in 1924. *Below left:* A cutout bookmark advertised the Jean Gros marionette production of *The Magical Land of Oz* (1928).

The Tin Woodman of the Magical Land of Oz announces JEAN GROS FRENCH MARIONETTES

THE SCARECROW OF OZ

ANSWERS QUESTIONS BY RADIO

THE SCARECROW OF OZ

Despite its astounding dullness, the 1925 Chadwick film of *The Wizard of Oz* was given maximum publicity. *Left:* The dust jacketed copy of a special edition of the book, illustrated with eight stills from the picture. *Right:* A glass advertising slide, designed for projection between feature films at theaters due to play the Chadwick show. *Above:* Original preliminary poster art for the film's Swedish release.

M. DeLange présente : **ZIGOTO** dans
LE SORCIER D'OZ
LE FILM COMIQUE LE PLUS FANTASTIQUE

Though planned as a showcase for director/star Larry Semon, the 1925 *Wizard* is notable today only for its casting of the pre-Stan Laurel Oliver Hardy in the role of a Kansas farmhand who briefly disguises himself as a Tin Woodman. *Above:* Mini-poster for the French release of the film showing Semon as the Scarecrow. *Left:* A hard-colored lobby card, featuring (from left) Hardy, G. Howe Black as another Kansas farmhand, Charles Murray as the Wizard, and Semon. (Nepotism note: Dorothy was played by Semon's wife, Dorothy Dwan.)

59

REACTS ON TOTO

He chases his tail, then performs the same
business as Dorothy; looking around behind
him to say who the lovely lady can be talking
about. Of course there is nothing behind him,
so he makes a little circle and, turning,
looks back up at Dorothy questioningly.

GROUP SHOT - DOROTHY - WITCH - TOTO

Dorothy   Dorothy (laughing)
           Who, me?

           Witch (musing)
Now, I'm a little mixed up because a new witch has
just dropped a house on the Wicked Witch of the
East -- and that's the house on the -- and here you are -
and that's all that's left of the Witch.

(Dorothy points and we CUT IN A QUICK CLOSEUP
of two ruby shoes sticking out from under
the house)

Witch   Olinda
Then the Munchkins want to know is: are you
a good witch or a bad witch?

           Dorothy
Why, I'm not any witch at all... I'm Dorothy
Gale from Kansas.

(There is a musical peal of laughter
from behind the bushes and flowers.
Dorothy sees them)

           Olinda
           They're laughing because I'm a
           witch. I'm Olinda, the Witch of the North.

           Dorothy
Oh... You are? I beg your pardon. But I've never
heard of a beautiful witch.

           Olinda
Only bad witches are ugly. It's only bad

(again the musical laughter comes again from
the mountains and are beginning to
come out from cover)
They're laughing because they're so happy you've
set them free, and because they're so happy you're
really one of the witch for them. You're really
the Munchkin's national heroine, my dear.

                                          CONTINUED:

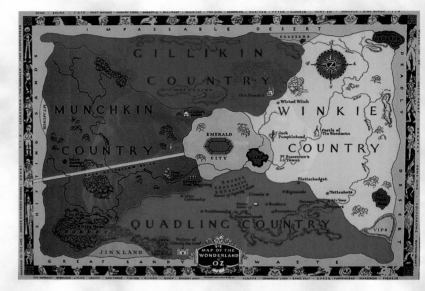

Even as America slid into the Depression, Oz maintained an all-encompassing hold on its public. The Yellow Brick Road provided any traveler the same momentary escape from tribulation as that supplied by the then-prevalent, kaleidoscopic film musical numbers of Busby Berkeley. More than just a diversion, however, Oz had become an established tangibility; for millions, it was "real." In casual but salient prose, Ruth Plumly Thompson offered, "A child who may not be able to name offhand the capital of Nebraska or Montana can tell you in a flash the capital of Oz and is often more familiar with its principal rivers, mountains, rulers, points of interest, and historical landmarks than with those of his native state — perhaps because he considers Oz his native state."

While there was some sly and happy self-promotion in her statement, Thompson's "take" was soundly based on the thousands of fan letters she received while deep into a second decade as Royal Historian. Despite the financial vagaries of the times, the Thompson/Neill/Reilly & Lee triumvirate maintained its tradition: there was a new Oz book every year. The series remained the foundation of the phenomenon, and neither author nor illustrator ever flagged in the resourceful addition of eccentrics and escapades to the Ozian landscape.

There was additional Oz promotion as well. In 1932, Reilly & Lee reissued some of Baum's "Little Wizard Stories," capitalizing on a new national craze by repackaging them with jigsaw puzzles of Neill

illustrations. A comic serial appeared at the same time, syndicated first to newspapers and then reprinted in comic books. In 1933, enormous statues of the Scarecrow and Tin Woodman were an integral feature of the "Enchanted Island" attraction at the Chicago World's Fair.

The only havoc was caused when Whitman issued *The Laughing Dragon of Oz* (1935), a "Big Little Book" written by Baum's son, Frank Joslyn. Reilly & Lee brought suit; their contract with Baum's widow gave them publishing rights to any Oz sequels. Whitman quickly agreed to let the book drift out of print and abandoned plans for a second title, *The Enchanted Princess of Oz*.

Meanwhile, authorized dramatizations continued to emerge. The Meglin Kiddies, a troupe of Los Angeles-area performing children, appeared in a two-reel *The Land of Oz* film in 1933. That same year, Ted Eshbaugh produced a brief, animated *The Wizard of Oz*, historically notable for the fact that the opening Kansas sequence was tinted only in shades of black-and-white and blue; when Dorothy and Toto fell out of a cyclonic sky into Oz, they and their surroundings suddenly

Preceding pages: MGM's *The Wizard of Oz.* An early script by Florence Ryerson and Edgar Allan Woolf; an Adrian apron tested (but not used) by Judy Garland; and the blouse she wore during the first two weeks of filming. (That footage was scrapped, and a new costume was fashioned for her.)

Above: "The Wonderland of Oz" map, distributed as a premium for the 1932-1933 newspaper cartoon serial.

evolved into Technicolor. The most far-reaching (if short-lived) Ozian reenactment was delivered directly into millions of homes when the National Broadcasting Company brought adaptations of the first six Oz books to radio. There were three, "live" fifteen-minute shows per week from September 25, 1933 through March 23, 1934, and each opened with the portentous words of announcer Ben Grauer: "Jell-O presents *The Wizard of Oz*!"

But every preceding (and, as it turned out, subsequent) Oz dramatic adaptation would fade into comparative obscurity with the 1939 release of MGM's Technicolor motion picture. There had been years of conjecture about a possible Oz feature — for Eddie Cantor as the Scarecrow, for W. C. Fields as the Wizard, for Mary Pickford, Helen Hayes, Shirley Temple, or Marcia Mae Jones as Dorothy. But only MGM could risk $3.2 million and manifest the resources (on either side of the camera) for a live-action fantasy. Their *The Wizard of Oz* was envisioned both as a showcase for fast-rising sixteen-year-old contract player Judy Garland and as an "integrated" film musical, in which songs and dances were an inherent part of the storytelling process.

Fraught with script, concept, casting, and production delays, the Victor Fleming/Mervyn LeRoy/Arthur Freed production took — from proposal to premiere — nearly two years to realize. Plans for its promotion induced MGM to establish a corporate merchandising force; they realized only limited success in their initial efforts but nevertheless licensed more than a score of Oz products.

The finished film itself knew few limitations: it broke attendance records across the nation and won mostly euphoric reviews. (One or two of the few dissenting critics were subsequently, publicly taken to task by their fellow journalists.) And even though its status as a legend and icon was decades in the future, nothing apart from Baum's original book would have more ultimate importance and resonance in the first one hundred years of Oz than MGM's *Wizard*.

Above: The cover for the giveaway scrapbook provided to children who wanted to clip, mount, and save "The Wonderland of Oz" comic strips.

Above: A 1939 trade paper ad for the MGM film premiere and a bag of "magic sand from along the yellow brick road," given away in theater lobbies to promote the film.

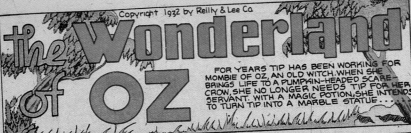

This circular, right, was sent to newspapers to solicit syndication contracts for "The Wonderland of Oz." *Left:* Some of the 443 strips were later adapted for use as comic book serials. *Below:* Reilly & Lee boxed four of Baum's "Little Wizard Stories" with jigsaw puzzles in 1932.

In 1933–1934, Jell-O promotional pages, left, were added to the four "Little Wizard" booklets and given as premiums for the NBC Oz radio series. *Right:* The back cover of a Jell-O booklet.

Ellen van Volkenburg produced a much-admired marionette version, above, of *The Wizard of Oz* via the Cornish Players of Seattle in 1934. *Left:* The Scarecrow can be seen as one of the engraved characters on this collectible key from the 1933 World's Fair "Enchanted Island." The key rests on the cover of *A Beautiful Model of the Enchanted Island*, a do-it-yourself-kit and souvenir of the fair. *Bottom left:* A cut-out representation of the Island's Tin Woodman statue from the same book.

Dorothy and Toto hand puppets, above, designed in connection with a WPA Museum project in 1932.

To tie in with a contemporary publishing fad, Bobbs-Merrill licensed a 1934 Waddle Book edition of *The Wizard of Oz,* which included bound-in cardboard cutouts of *Oz* characters who could be detached and assembled to walk down an accompanying "Yellow Brick" ramp. *Below left:* The Waddle-Book cover.

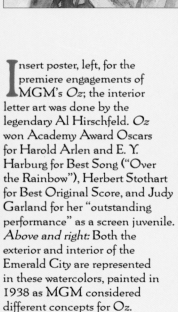

Insert poster, left, for the premiere engagements of MGM's *Oz*; the interior letter art was done by the legendary Al Hirschfeld. *Oz* won Academy Award Oscars for Harold Arlen and E. Y. Harburg for Best Song ("Over the Rainbow"), Herbert Stothart for Best Original Score, and Judy Garland for her "outstanding performance" as a screen juvenile. *Above and right:* Both the exterior and interior of the Emerald City are represented in these watercolors, painted in 1938 as MGM considered different concepts for *Oz*.

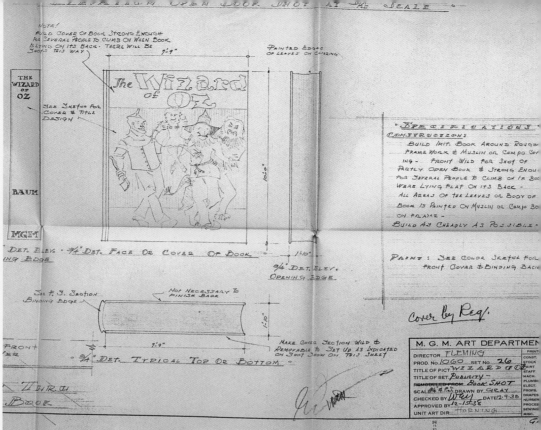

A detail of the studio blue-print, right, for the oversized Oz book used in publicity photos with the cast (such as that shown above). *Below right:* A detail of the studio blueprint for "Professor Marvel's Wagon." *Below:* "The Parents Magazine Medal Awarded to The Wizard of Oz/The Movie of the Month for Family Audiences/ September 1939." (In 1998, *Oz* would be ranked sixth on the American Film Institute's list of The 100 Best American Movies.)

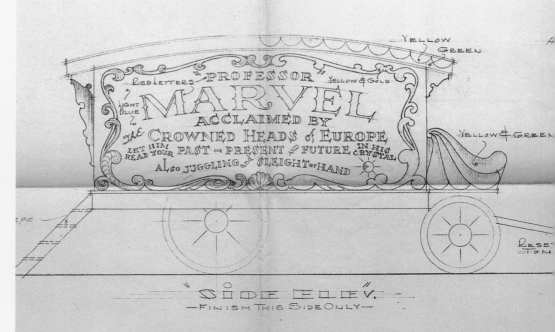

"You see that? That's how much longer you've got to be alive."

As the epitome of villainy, Margaret Hamilton threatened the life of Judy Garland with this hourglass. In the last thirty years, MGM's *Oz* props and costumes have set record prices at auction.

Only around a dozen actors were actually costumed and "flew" as Winged Monkeys in MGM's *Oz*; scores more were created as eight-inch rubber miniatures and manipulated like puppets. *Right:* One of the few surviving monkey miniatures, inset on a scene still of the "Jitter Forest" where they first attacked Dorothy and her friends.

"Now the charm began to work. The sky was darkened, and a low rumbling sound was heard in the air. There was a rushing of many wings; a great chattering and laughing; and the sun came out of the dark sky to show the Wicked Witch surrounded by a crowd of Monkeys, each with a pair of immense and powerful wings on his shoulders."

"You are welcome, most noble Sorceress, to the land of the Munchkins. We are so grateful to you for having killed the Wicked Witch of the East, and for setting our people free from bondage."

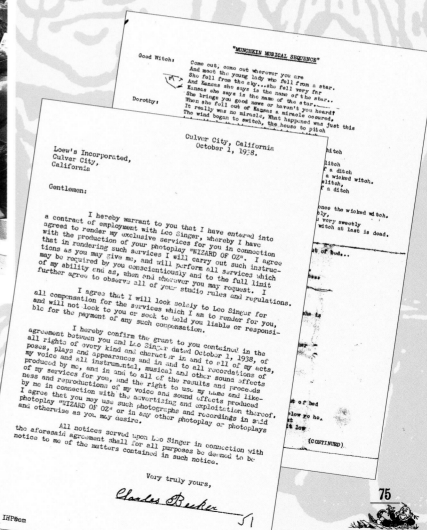

The original handmade heavy felt costume, left, worn by Jerry Maren, central member of "The Lollipop Guild" trio. *Above:* Autographed Maren photo, showing his presentation of a Munchkinland souvenir to Judy Garland. *Right:* Work agreement signed by "Munchkin Mayor" Charles Becker, and the lyric sheet distributed at rehearsal to the 124 "little people" of *Oz* so that they could memorize the words to the "Munchkin Musical Sequence."

"MUNCHKIN MUSICAL SEQUENCE"

Good Witch:
Come out, come out wherever you are
And meet the young lady who fell from a star.
She fell from the sky...she fell very far
And Kansas she says is the name of the star..
Kansas she says is the name of the star.___

Dorothy:
She brings you good news or haven't you heard?
When she fell out of Kansas a miracle occured.
It really was no miracle, What happened was just this
The wind began to switch, the house to pitch

Culver City, California
October 1, 1938.

Loew's Incorporated,
Culver City,
California.

Gentlemen:

I hereby warrant to you that I have entered into a contract of employment with Leo Singer, whereby I have agreed to render my exclusive services for you in connection with the production of your photoplay "WIZARD OF OZ". I agree that in rendering such services I will carry out such instructions as you may give me, and will perform all services which may be required by you conscientiously and to the full limit of my ability and as, when and wherever you may request. I further agree to observe all of your studio rules and regulations.

I agree that I will look solely to Leo Singer for all compensation for the services which I am to render for you, and will not look to you or seek to hold you liable or responsible for the payment of any such compensation.

I hereby confirm the grant to you contained in the agreement between you and Leo Singer dated October 1, 1938, of all rights of every kind and character in and to all of my acts, poses, plays and appearances and in and to all recordings of my voice and all instrumental, musical and other sound effects produced by me, and in and to all of the results and proceeds of my services for you, and the right to use my name and likeness and reproductions of my voice and sound effects produced by me in connection with the advertising and exploitation thereof. I agree that you may use such photographs and recordings in said photoplay "WIZARD OF OZ" or in any other photoplay or photoplays and otherwise as you may desire.

All notices served upon Leo Singer in connection with the aforesaid agreement shall for all purposes be deemed to be notice to me of the matters contained in such notice.

Very truly yours,

Charles Becker

IHP:em

The Dart Board Equipment Company box cover and game board for their 1939 tie-in to *The Wizard of Oz* film. The product was never mass-manufactured, and only a few test samples are known to exist. Even the readily available Oz merchandise licensed by MGM enjoyed but a limited shelf life, as it was so specifically aligned to theatrical bookings for the film (which ran from August 1939 until early 1940).

In 1939, the Ideal Novelty & Toy Company issued thirteen-inch, fifteen-and-a-half-inch, and eighteen-inch "Judy Garland as Dorothy" dolls and seventeen-inch and twenty-one-inch "The Strawman by Ray Bolger" dolls. This is the mid-size Judy; the larger Bolger is positioned above her. Each of the four smaller Scarecrows shown here boasts variant clothing.

"One of the big trees had been partly chopped through, and standing beside it, with an uplifted axe in his hands, was a man made entirely of tin. His head and arms and legs were jointed upon his body, but he stood perfectly motionless, as if he could not stir at all."

The Kerk Guild manufactured this boxed set of five "Soapy Characters from the Land of Oz" as an MGM tie-in in 1939.

The British Hutchinson & Company "movie edition" of *The Wizard of Oz* (1940), above, included hand-colored stills as illustrations and a similarly adapted wrap-around dust jacket. *Left:* A glass slide that movie houses could project to promote *Oz* as a forthcoming attraction. *Right:* One of a dozen Oz Valentines issued in 1940 and 1941 by the American Colortype Company.

Drawings of scenes from the *Oz* film, top left, decorate this Brian Fabrics scarf. *Above:* Although Corning Glassworks manufactured several *Oz* glasses as premiums for Sealtest Cottage Cheese, this Judy Garland prototype was never commercially marketed; it may have been envisioned as part of a second series. *Left:* The box cover and one of the "Hangers from The Merrie Land of Oz," manufactured by Barney Stempler & Sons.

1940s

OZ
AROUND
THE
WORLD

The *Wizard of Oz* was one of the top-grossing films of 1939 and an Academy Award-nominee for Best Picture. In the annual *Film Daily* poll of more than 450 critics, it ranked among the ten best movies of the year. But due to an odd combination of factors, MGM's musical lost about $750,000 in its initial release. Though theaters enjoyed turn-away business, around two-thirds of the *Oz* audience was comprised of children, who paid substantially less admission than did adults. The glut of incoming, pre-booked film product often meant that *Oz* couldn't be held over in many cities, even though attendance warranted extended engagements. Most detrimental to its income, however, was the loss of much of the potential foreign market; World War II began in Europe in September 1939, two weeks after the American *Oz* premiere.

While some foreign countries were able to exhibit *Oz* in 1940, many others had to wait until after the war was over in 1945. But whenever it was finally seen, the film provided literary inspiration around the world: the 1940s marked the first regular appearance of *Oz* books in foreign languages. A few of them were based on (or at least illustrated by) material from the film. The vast majority were straightforward translations or adaptations of the original Baum story. No matter their source, however, the books proved (and remain) fascinating primarily because of their artwork. The characters and countrysides of *Oz* continually provoked a spectrum of wildly diverse illustrative concepts.

The 1940s also brought changes and disruptions in the American *Oz* book series for the first time in two decades. Ruth Plumly Thompson wrote her nineteenth volume in 1939; *Ozoplaning with the Wizard of Oz* was titled to tie in with the MGM film. She then "resigned" from her post as Royal Historian, feeling at least momentarily drained by her long-term commitment to the series and its fans. For the sake of continuity, Reilly & Lee approached John R. Neill to both author and illustrate the *Oz* book for 1940. His writing — though flamboyant

Preceding pages: Detail from a Spanish poster for *El Mago de Oz* (1945).

Above left: Swedish poster (1940). *Above right:* Cover of an illustrated program for the Austrian release of *Oz* (1940).

and inventive — was only partially as successful as his draftsmanship, but he contributed three titles in all before his death in 1943. At that point, the publishers put the series on hiatus until after the war; in 1946 and 1949, they issued manuscripts written by Jack Snow, a lifelong Baum aficionado and scholar. Though well-crafted, Snow's stories lacked humor; the illustrations by Frank Kramer were affable, though missing the beauty and finer touches of Neill's work. Both books sold less well than had the earlier titles, and Reilly & Lee felt the series might well have run its course.

Oz nonetheless remained in the nation's consciousness. There were a few new product tie-ins (most notably its association with Swift's peanut butter "spread") and, even though the MGM film disappeared from theaters after second- and third-run engagements in 1940, its songs continued to grow in popularity. MGM first made the *Oz* musical score and orchestrations available to the St. Louis Muny Opera for a summer theater production of *The Wizard* in 1942. Other professional theaters around the world soon clamored for the chance to

Left: "The Wizard of Oz Card Game" from London's Castell Brothers Ltd. (1940). *Right:* Italian poster (1947).

JUDY **GARLAND**
Frank **MORGAN**

in **TECHNICOLOR**

il MAGO di OZ

PRODOTTO DA MERVYN LE ROY   *Regia:* VICTOR FLEMING

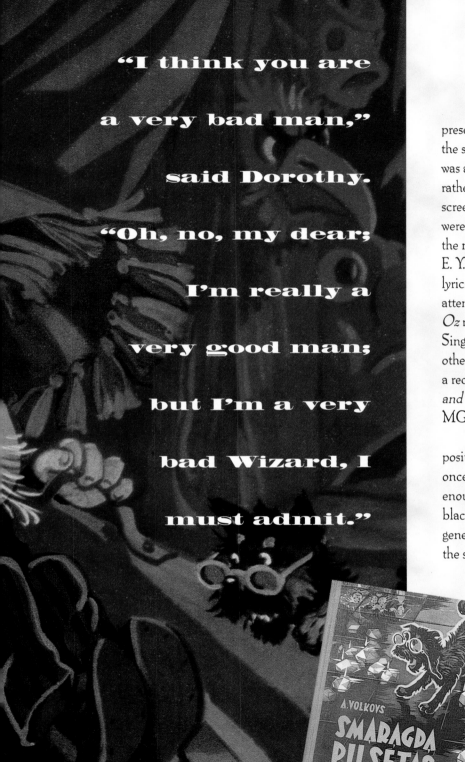

"I think you are a very bad man," said Dorothy.

"Oh, no, my dear; I'm really a very good man; but I'm a very bad Wizard, I must admit."

present *Oz* on stage. Although the script of those early versions was adapted from Baum's book rather than from the film screenplay, the songs throughout were primarily those written for the movie by Harold Arlen and E. Y. Harburg. Their music and lyrics had first enjoyed special attention in 1939 when Decca released a set of 78-rpm *Oz* records featuring Judy Garland and the Ken Darby Singers. This was available throughout the 1940s, as were other renditions of the *Oz* score. In 1949, Capitol issued a record album based on Baum's fourth title, *Dorothy and the Wizard in Oz*; it was a clever marketing move, as MGM that year reissued *The Wizard of Oz*.

The re-release was a triumph for the studio, proof positive that a market existed for classic older films. *Oz* once again garnered superlative reviews and took in enough at the box office to put the picture firmly in the black. Its reappearance was also a cheerful reminder of general *Oz* omnipresence, even if public sensibility about the series had settled into second-nature comfortability.

As it turned out, both the film and the book on which it was based were on the brink of a genuinely colossal resurgence. The second half of the century would see *Oz* explode into public consciousness as had no other American fairy tale or motion picture — and ultimately command a plateau of singular, unparalleled prominence.

Left: Illustration and cover from a 1962 Latvian edition of *The Wizard of Oz*, a prime example of the surge of foreign *Oz* books that began in the 1940s and never abated. *Above:* French film magazine for August 1939, promoting the forthcoming *Oz* film.

"Lily habitait avec son oncle Henry, qui était fermier, et sa tante Anna, qui était la femme du fermier, dans une maison au milieu d'une grande, grande plaine, dans l'Arkansas, en Amérique."

– Chapitre Premier, *Le Magicien D'Ohz*, 1932 (the first foreign translation, in which Dorothy was named Lily and lived in Arkansas)

With the gradual widespread international exhibition of MGM's *Oz*, several editions of the book capitalized on the film characters, including: *O Feiticeiro de Oz* (Portugal, 1946), *Trollkarlen fran Oz* (Sweden, 1940), and *Il Mago di Oz* (Italy, 1947).

THE ORIGINAL OZ BOOK

The WIZARD OF OZ by L. FRANK BAUM

Illustrated by EVELYN COPELMAN

adapted from the famous pictures by

W. W. DENSLOW

In 1944, the original Denslow artwork was dropped from *The Wizard of Oz,* and publisher Bobbs-Merrill had new pictures drawn by Evelyn Copelman. Her concepts, vastly different than Denslow's, were inspired to a great extent by the MGM film. Countless copies of the Copelman-illustrated *Wizard* have since been printed; her work remains among the most familiar and treasured of any Oz artist. *Below:* The stationery used by two Royal Historians.

Office of
The Royal Historian of Oz
RUTH PLUMLY THOMPSON

JACK SNOW

Royal Historian of Oz

The only known copy of the glorious two-panel billboard for the MGM film, *left*, designed in France by preeminent contemporary poster artist, "Grinsson" (1940). *Above:* Hirschfeld art and film photographs highlight this *Oz* stationery, distributed by MGM for in-house and promotional use in (at least) English and Spanish.

The Oz "Model-Craft" kit, right, was available during the 1940s and 1950s, enabling children to mold and paint their own Oz figurines. *Above:* The Capitol Records adaptation of Baum's fourth Oz book was conceived and illustrated to cash in on the 1949 U.S. reissue of the MGM film. *Far right:* The cover of MGM's 1949 record, in which an orchestra and chorus re-created the movie songs.

METROSCOPE

THE

WIZARD OF OZ

Judy **GARLAND**
Frank **MORGAN**
Ray **BOLGER**
Bert **LAHR**
Jack **HALEY**

BILLIE BURKE · MARGARET HAMILTON
CHARLEY GRAPEWIN · AND THE MUNCHKINS
A VICTOR FLEMING Production
Screenplay by Noel Langley · Florence Ryerson
and Edgar Alan Woolf
Produced by MERVYN LEROY

It's
METRO-GOLDWYN-MAYER'S
TECHNICOLOR TRIUMPH!

After their first exposure to *The Wizard of Oz* via the 1949 MGM reissue, millions of children manifested the same ardor as had their parents — and grandparents. Consequently, 1950-1952 saw a proliferation of publications for youngsters: a picture-book abridgement, Oz additions to the Little Golden and Wonder Books series, and even a new title from Reilly & Lee. In 1951, they issued Rachel Cosgrove's *The Hidden Valley of Oz* which, in best Baum tradition, sent an American child soaring through the air (this time via runaway kite) to an eventual denouement in the Emerald City. Jack Snow returned to the post of Royal Historian three years later and assembled profiles of more than six hundred Oz characters for *Who's Who in Oz.* Though a sales disappointment (faithful readers sought a story, not an encyclopedia), the book was indication of both the scope and believability of all that had been wrought by Baum and Company since 1900.

In 1956, Oz won further respect when the Columbia University Libraries paid homage to Baum's centennial in a resplendent exhibition of his work. That same year, the copyright expired on *The Wizard of Oz*, which meant an astronomical new level of visibility for the first Oz book. Though sales figures for past printings already topped four million copies, its public domain status meant that anyone could produce a new edition of the story or utilize its characters; a parade of products began immediately.

It was a propitious time for such excitement; those who cared about Oz were about to be aggressively challenged. For decades, there had been a pointed antipathy to fantasy from scattered librarians, educators, and historians. (Their limited perspective was dryly summarized by author Martin Gardner: "How could anything so popular, they say to themselves, be anything but trash? Of course it never occurs to them to *read* an Oz book and decide for themselves.") The negative

Preceding pages: Glasses, pails, and a character mobile promote Swift's Oz Peanut Butter. First made available as "peanut spread" in 1940, the product was marketed well into the 1970s in various collectible containers.

Above: A poster for the 1955 British reissue of the MGM film featured a photograph of the adult Judy Garland to appeal to her contemporary audience.

faction sank to its all-time low in 1957. Echoing the disdain of compatriots in Florida and Washington, D.C., the director of the Detroit library system publicly announced there was "nothing uplifting or elevating" about Baum's work; he accused the Oz books of "negativism" and a "cowardly approach to life." Oz books were summarily banned from the shelves of some libraries — if they had carried them at all.

In response, there was for the first time a figurative rush to the Ozzy barricades by prestigious journalists, teachers, and more knowledgeable librarians; the public outcry was enough to effect (if gradually) the reinstatement — and even further recognition — of all things Oz. As Gardner later reported, "Oz fans [began] to cry out against this conspiracy . . . and to say, without being in the least ashamed, that the Royal History is a great and enduring work of American Literature." He and Russell Nye coauthored a 1957 appreciation of Baum, *The Wizard of Oz and Who He Was*; it was just the first of many successful volleys from esteemed writers that either educated or muzzled any non-fans.

Perhaps the fervor of 1957 was impelled by what in retrospect would be the most significant event of the preceding year: the television premiere of the MGM film. A second theatrical reissue in 1955 had been unevenly

promoted, but its limited success meant nothing when the TV ratings were posted for November 3, 1956; more than forty-five million people had been spellbound for two hours. Few families could then boast a color set, and most viewers saw the picture in black and white. But even under those conditions, the film had found a new home.

The TV host that evening was the Cowardly Lion himself, Bert Lahr, and he was joined in emcee duties by the "daughter of Dorothy," ten-year-old Liza Minnelli.

Above: This theater program accompanied the first appearance of MGM's *Oz* in Japanese theaters (1955) and provided a synopsis of the plot along with stills and artwork.

("Mama" Judy watched on a backstage TV at Broadway's Palace Theater where she was starring in her own show.) A more significant on-camera presence, however, was that of an Oz collector from Brooklyn, whom the producers remembered from publicity he'd received as a contributor to the Columbia exhibition. They invited him — and his first edition of *The Wizard* — to appear with Lahr and Minnelli; Justin Schiller was just thirteen years old.

Two months later, that same indefatigable teen channeled his enthusiasm into the formation of The International Wizard of Oz Club, with sixteen charter members (most much older than he) and a four-page, mimeographed "newspaper" ingenuously titled *The Baum Bugle*. It was quiet indication of Ozmania-to-come; by 1999, the club had become the preeminent Oz fan base, and the *Bugle* was a professionally designed magazine with thousands of annual subscribers.

Above: MGM issued its first *Oz* soundtrack album in conjunction with the film's television debut in November 1956. Ultimately a perennial best-seller, the album combined songs and dialogue lifted directly from the film print — an innovation for that time. *Right:* Endpapers for the 1950 Random House picture-book adaptation of *Oz* with evocative illustrations by Anton Loeb. In print for more than two decades, this edition provided the initial introduction to the story for many younger children.

This book belongs to

"The road to the City of Emeralds is paved with yellow brick," said the Witch; "so you cannot miss it. When you get to Oz, do not be afraid of him, but tell your story and ask him to help you."

When *The Wizard of Oz* book passed into public domain in 1956, Oz became more and more visible in the marketplace. *Far left:* Detail of Ozzy fabric from a woman's dress. *Above left:* Visual retellings of the story included the oft-repackaged View-Master treatment (beginning in 1957) and extended to — among others — *The Wiz* in 1978. *Below:* Swift's Peanut Butter publicity began with large product pails in the 1940s. By the 1950s, the company was also providing decorated glasses, promotional pens, recipe suggestions, and a coloring book.

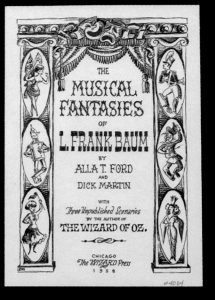

Original art, above, by Dick Martin for the title page of *The Musical Fantasies of L. Frank Baum* (1958), here inscribed to his coauthor, Alla T. Ford. *Right:* Catalog for the 1956 Baum Centenary Exhibition. *Below: Bibliographia Oziana* and two issues of *The Baum Bugle* — samples of the important work done by The International Wizard of Oz Club since 1957; spearhead of the group for more than three decades was Secretary Fred M. Meyer. *Far right:* Newspaper ad art for the third national telecast of MGM's *Oz*. CBS initially used its own network series' stars and their children to emcee the program; shown at top left are the 1960 hosts, Richard ("Have Gun, Will Travel") Boone and son Peter .

TV WEEK

COMPLETE TV RADIO LISTINGS

DECEMBER 11, 1960

AUM

'Wizard of Oz'

STORY — PAGE 29

Richard Boone and son Peter, age 7 (left) are hosts of the color film on Ch 7 today (Sunday) from 6 to 8 p.m. Do you recognize Judy Garland, Ray Bolger, Jack Haley, Frank Morgan, Bert Lahr and Billie Burke?

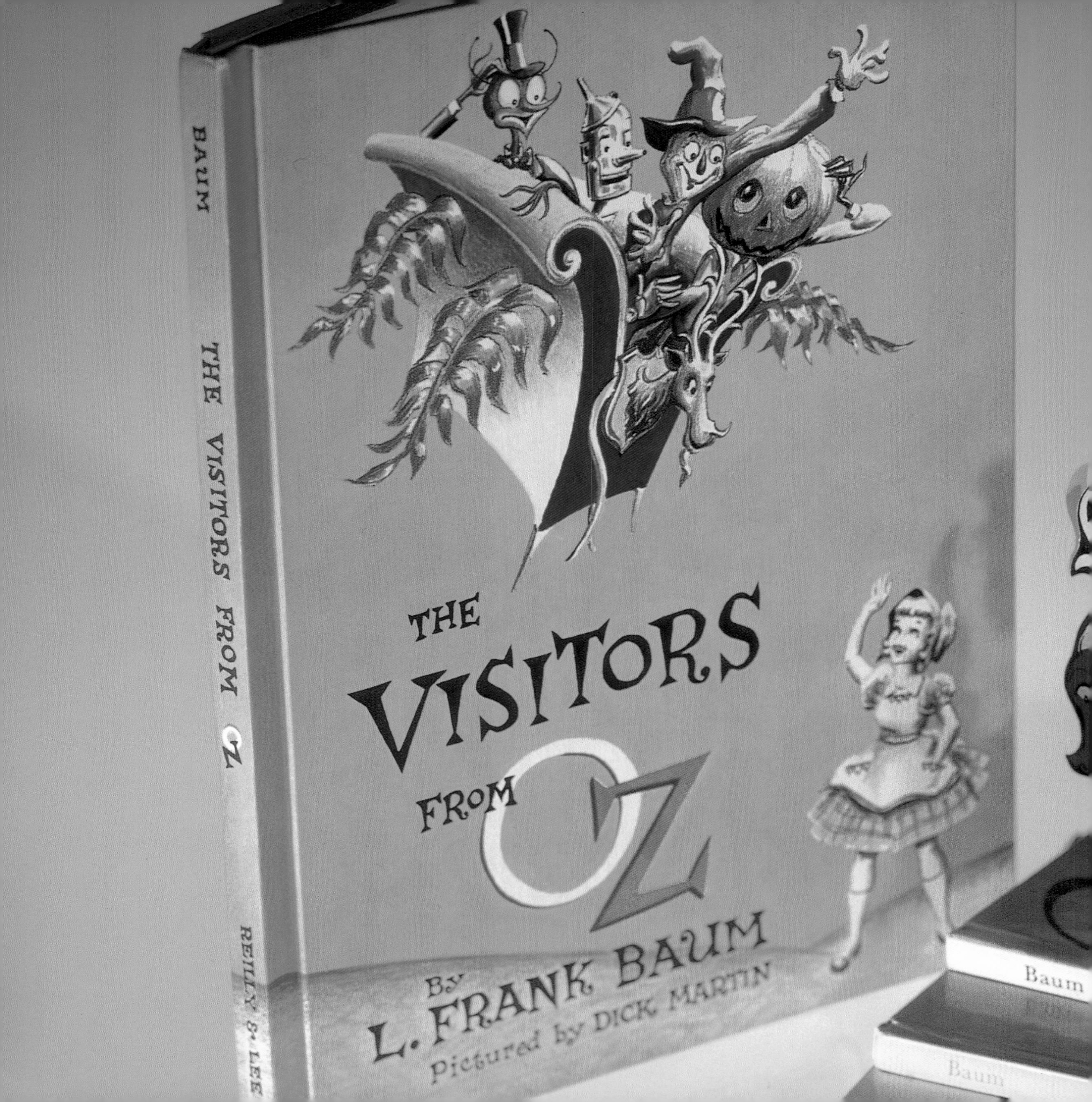
BAUM
THE VISITORS FROM OZ
REILLY & LEE
THE VISITORS FROM OZ
By L. FRANK BAUM
Pictured by DICK MARTIN
Baum
Baum

OFF TO SEE THE WIZARD

THEY'RE HERE!

THE VISITORS FROM OZ

Left: Oz books with new Dick Martin dust jackets (1960) and Progressive Art Products bookends (1971).

Martin, whose bright drawings or designs had become an irrevocable part of literally every Regnery/Oz project.

The general furor also brought about fresh examinations of Baum's life work in publications as diverse as *American Heritage, The Reader's Digest,* and *The American Book Collector.* Majority opinion throughout was not only sympathetic but often downright laudatory in the long-delinquent acknowledgment that America had possessed in Frank Baum its own Hans Christian Andersen or Brothers Grimm.

Equally enthusiastic was the media attention paid to an ever-more-active International Wizard of Oz Club. When their annual "Oz Convention" was described in a casual *Saturday Review* column in 1963, the notice brought in scores of new members, as did much of the ensuing journalistic scrutiny of their endeavors. Such consideration was warranted, for the Club quite often stood at the forefront of any developing Oz enterprise. As their roster grew, they were able to augment *The Baum Bugle* with a publishing program of Oz maps, out-of-print books and rare Baum material, and a definitive bibliography of the complex printing history of the Oz series.

By now, several of those early Oz books were in the public domain; separately or coupled with the much-loved MGM movie songs, Baum's stories and characters

For all of its preceding fame, Oz now reached a new zenith of celebrity. The larger percentage of that renown was due to the MGM film; it enjoyed an unprecedented ten national telecasts between 1960-1970 and never placed lower than fourth in any weekly ratings poll. By mid-decade, children had come to anticipate the annual appearance of *The Wizard of Oz* as a family event on a par with their birthdays and Christmas.

Appropriately, the picture's popularity kindled an overall passion for the subject that revitalized every aspect of Oz. By happy coincidence, Henry Regnery had purchased Reilly & Lee in 1959; under his guidance, the company embarked on a vigorous marketing and promotional policy. Among other activities, they issued a full-length biography of Baum, adapted his 1904-1905 comic strip into a deluxe *The Visitors From Oz* volume, brought out picture books of four of his Oz stories, and added a fortieth title — *Merry Go Round in Oz* (1963) — to the official series. The latter was written by the distinguished children's author Eloise Jarvis McGraw (with considerable input from her daughter, Lauren Lynn); it was illustrated by lifelong Baum devotee, Dick

Preceding pages: The "flying machine" Gump was re-created as an assembled paper cutout by Dick Martin to promote *The Visitors From Oz* (1960); the next year, he illustrated four Oz picture books.

Below: The Wizard of Oz as read in Russia (1961) and Israel (1963).

thus figured prominently in dramatic presentations throughout the 1960s. Their venues ranged from ice shows and the circus to puppet plays and television programs. Shirley Temple played both Princess Ozma and her alter ego (an enchanted lad named Tip) in an hour-long NBC teleplay of *The Land of Oz* in 1960. A year later, Alfred Rankin and Jules Bass debuted 130 five-minute "Tales of The Wizard of Oz" cartoons, which ran in syndication throughout North America. They further parlayed their Oz connection into a much-publicized (albeit poorly received) NBC animated special, *Return to Oz* in 1964. As early as 1961, there had been preliminary negotiations for an MGM cartoon series in which Judy Garland would vocally re-create the role of Dorothy Gale. Instead, the studio later produced "Off To See the Wizard," which utilized their own animated Oz characters as hosts of weekly family film fare over ABC-TV in 1967-1968.

Such nonstop multimedia activity also resulted in the most massive amount of Oz merchandising to that time. Though many products were related to the various TV shows, even random Oz ware began to hit the marketplace with increasing regularity. In

1969, exploitation emerged on its grandest scale with the opening of a "Land of Oz" theme park near Banner Elk, North Carolina. Though much off the regular tourist beat and comparatively inaccessible near the summit of Beech Mountain, the park still managed to draw enthralled children and their families who thrilled to an adventure tour much inspired by the MGM film.

Perhaps the most telling measure of the force of Oz in the 1960s is that its happily emotional resonance continued to grow and affect all ages — despite increasing societal turmoil and world unrest. The premature death of Judy Garland in June 1969 provided a poignant underscoring to the innocence and importance of Baum's story; a world "where there isn't any trouble ... somewhere over the rainbow" was perhaps more to be desired, more a necessary haven to be treasured than ever before.

Above left and right: Curad bandages and a Mattel jack-in-the-box were among many products tied in to the "Off to See the Wizard" series (1967).

Above: A Reilly & Lee map of Oz, designed by Dick Martin to promote new hardcover editions of the fourteen Baum Oz titles in 1964-1965.

Books about Baum and Oz, above, began with *Utopia Americana* (1929), continued with *The Wizard of Oz and Who He Was* (1957) and *The Musical Fantasies of L. Frank Baum* (1958), and peaked with *To Please A Child* (1961), the latter coauthored by journalist Russell P. MacFall. The majestic *The Annotated Wizard of Oz* (1973) and a children's treatment, *L. Frank Baum* (1995), were among many subsequent accounts. *Above left: Merry Go Round in Oz* (1963), the new "white" editions of the Baum Oz books (1964–1965), and their respective promotional leaflets. *Left: The American Book Collector* devoted an entire issue to Baum in 1962. *Below: Oz* recordings proliferated throughout the decades as well, whether featuring MGM or original music, or the entire text of the first book. *Right:* Dick Martin's dazzling 1965 Oz book poster.

108

HERE ARE ALL YOUR OLD FRIENDS FROM THE MAGICAL LAND of OZ

Read All About Their AMAZING ADVENTURES in THE FAMOUS Z BOOKS

The REILLY & LEE Co. Publishers.

Dick Martin

PATCHWORK GIRL CAPTAIN SALT WOGGLE BUG LUCKY BUCKY NOME KING OJO MERRY GO ROUND

KABUMPO SILVER PRINCESS HANDY MANDY JACK PUMPKINHEAD SPEEDY SHAGGY MAN

"Come along,

Toto," she said,

"we will go to

the Emerald

City and ask

the great Oz how

to get back to

Kansas again."

The famous four as part of a Ringling Brothers circus divertissement (1965). *Below:* Prospectus and ad art for Shirley Temple's 1960–1961 TV series, which kicked off with an adaptation of the second Oz book. The cast included Agnes Moorehead, Jonathan Winters, Sterling Holloway, and Arthur Treacher. *Far right:* A felt pennant (1960) and souvenir program spread (1961–1962) for the Ice Capades' Oz production number.

THE
SHIRLEY
TEMPLE
SHOW

NBC TELEVISION NETWORK

1960-61

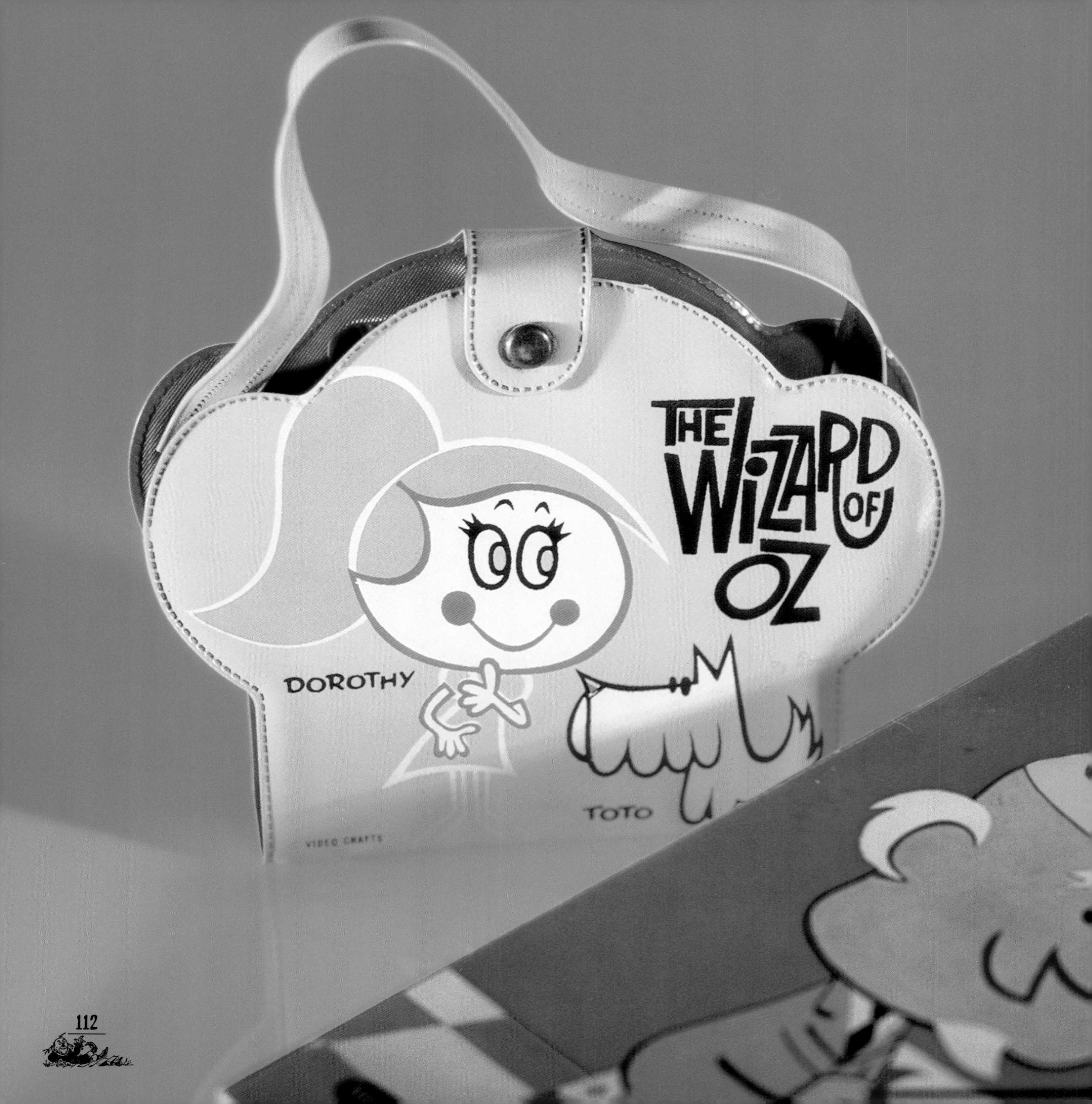
THE WIZZARD OF OZ
DOROTHY
TOTO
VIDEO CRAFTS

ERASES IN A WHIZ

WRITES LIKE MAGIC!

29¢
3012

AUTHORIZED EDITION
BASED ON THE NEW TV SERIES
TALES OF THE WIZARD OF OZ

© VIDEO CRAFTS, INC.

TO REMOVE STYLUS, SEE INSTRUCTIONS ON REVERSE SIDE

SAVES TIME

SAVES PAPER

SAVES PENCILS

GAMES

DOODLIN'

LOTS OF FUN

LIFT FILMS TO ERASE

MADE IN U.S.A.

The Rankin & Bass "Tales of The Wizard of Oz" cartoon series inspired a Ponytail coin purse, Whitman coloring book, and Lowe Company "Wizard Slate," among other products between 1961 and 1963. *Left:* An animation cel and matching background from their more ambitiously drawn *Return to Oz* TV special (1964).

TALES OF THE Wizard of Oz
COLORING BOOK

The Rankin & Bass *Return to Oz*, right, appeared briefly on videotape in 1986. The original 1964 telecast had been widely advertised by General Electric, which also offered a charm bracelet of the show's characters as a premium. Earlier in the 1960s, the Rankin & Bass "Tales of The Wizard of Oz" inspired Halco Oz Halloween masks and (at the far right) the Artistic Toy Company "Dandy Lion" and Dorothy dolls. *Above:* Program cover and the actual Dorothy marionette conceived by the renowned Bil Baird for his puppet retelling of *The Wizard of Oz,* which played off Broadway in 1968.

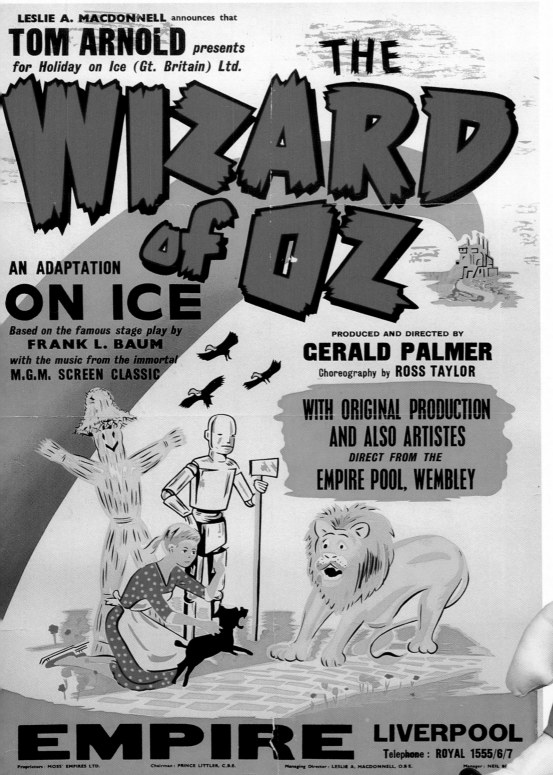

LESLIE A. MACDONNELL announces that

TOM ARNOLD presents

for Holiday on Ice (Gt. Britain) Ltd.

THE WIZARD of OZ

AN ADAPTATION
ON ICE

Based on the famous stage play by
FRANK L. BAUM
with the music from the immortal
M.G.M. SCREEN CLASSIC

PRODUCED AND DIRECTED BY
GERALD PALMER
Choreography by ROSS TAYLOR

WITH ORIGINAL PRODUCTION
AND ALSO ARTISTES
DIRECT FROM THE
EMPIRE POOL, WEMBLEY

EMPIRE LIVERPOOL
Telephone : ROYAL 1555/6/7

Proprietors: MOSS' EMPIRES LTD.   Chairman: PRINCE LITTLER, C.B.E.   Managing Director: LESLIE A. MACDONNELL, O.B.E.   Manager: NEIL B

Commencing TUESDAY, MAY 1ST - FOR 4 W

A full-production *Oz* ice show was first produced in the United Kingdom in 1962, foreshadowing by three decades a similar United States skating extravaganza.

talkin' "Patter™ Pillow" by mattel

OFF TO SEE THE WIZARD

I TALK!

Off-to-See
The Wizard SCARECROW

 MATTEL INC. TOYMAKERS   PULL TALK

ABC-TV's 1967–1968 "Off to See the Wizard" cartoon spawned merchandising on the largest scale to date. Among the licensed tie-ins: Mattel's talking puppets and Scarecrow pillow, three Louis Marx & Company windup "dancing toys," three Craft Master paint kits, four Multiple Toymakers "Rubb'r Nicks," and a set of Colorforms.

. . . they all followed him through the portal into the streets of the Emerald City.

117

"You see," the Scarecrow continued, confidentially, "I don't mind my legs and arms and body being stuffed, because I cannot get hurt. If anyone treads on my toes or sticks pins into me, it doesn't matter, for I can't feel it."

"No, my head is quite empty," answered the Woodman; "but once I had brains, and a heart also; so, having tried them both, I should much rather have a heart."

Oversized metal ornaments of two leading citizens of Oz for use in public parks. In the 1960s, this Tin Woodman was designed to top garbage cans; the Scarecrow served as a mid-board seesaw decoration.

"In the civilized countries I believe there are no witches left; nor wizards, nor sorceresses, nor magicians. But, you see, the Land of Oz has never been civilized, for we are cut off from all the rest of the world. Therefore we still have witches and wizards amongst us."

The Banner Elk "Land of Oz" theme park enjoyed a twelve-season run atop a mountain in North Carolina. It included a tour "through" Oz, displays of memorabilia, and the customary concession and souvenir stands; as shown here, the merchandise ran the gamut. A fire and dwindling attendance closed the park after the summer of 1980, but the site was reopened on a much more informal scale in the late 1990s.

Ceramic banks
of the MGM
characters from
Arnart Imports (circa
late 1960s).

"Do you think
Oz could give
me courage?"
asked the
Cowardly Lion.

"Just as easily
as he could give
me brains," said
the Scarecrow.

"Or give me a
heart," said the
Tin Woodman.

"Or send me back
to Kansas,"
said Dorothy.

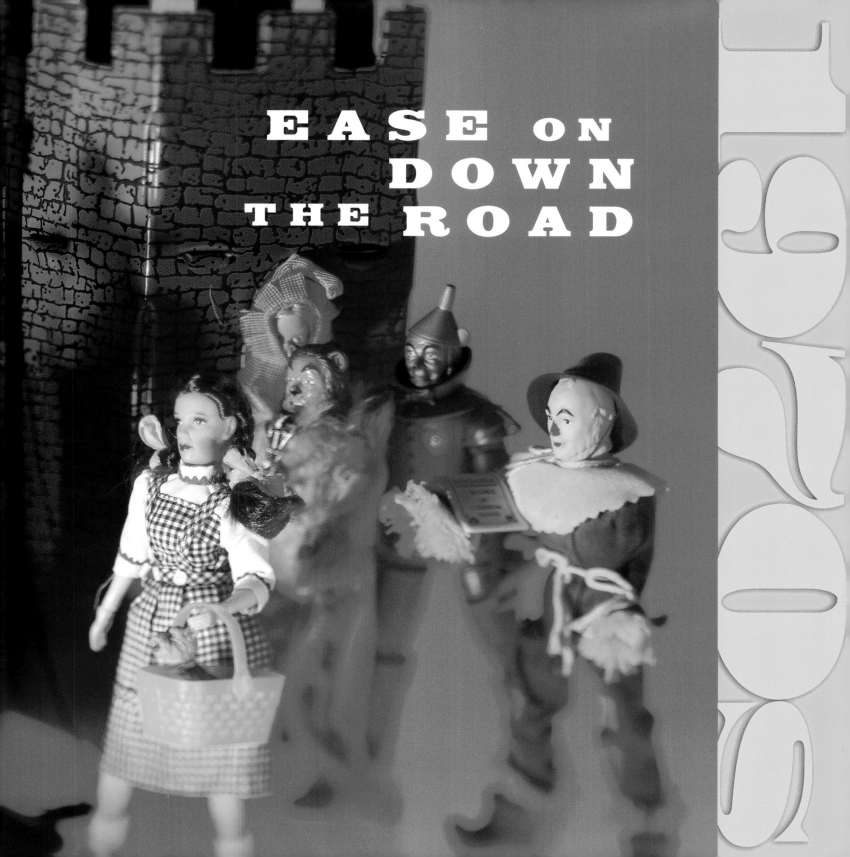

While the 1970s brought new Oz films, a smashingly successful Broadway musical, and a profusion of products and publications, MGM's *Wizard* continued to dominate the scene. Even a two-season theatrical reissue on a Saturday/Sunday matinee basis couldn't minimize its ongoing television success; by 1980, *Oz* had been shown twenty-two times — invariably as the top-rated program in its time slot. The 1970 telecast paid brief homage to the film's star when host Gregory Peck eulogized, "Judy Garland left a legacy of performances perhaps unequaled by any star of our time." When MGM auctioned its costumes and props later that year, the bid for Garland's ruby slippers topped all other sales at $15,000.

By now, the MGM treatment of *Oz* had become so ingrained in public consciousness that it was an integral part of daily American life. (Indeed, as early as 1970, it was estimated that more people had seen *Oz* than any other entertainment in history.) Parodies and paraphrases of its dialogue laced countless TV and film scripts, editorials, newscasts, and sermons. An accompanying acceleration in merchandising was thus inevitable and, whether MGM- or Baum-inspired, there were new coloring and comic books, collector's plates, Halloween costumes, figurines, découpage and toiletry kits — even a prototype bedroom suite of *Oz* furniture and fabric. The most notable new products arrived in 1975-1976 when Mego debuted their film-inspired *Oz* dolls and

accompanying playsets of the Emerald City, Witch's Castle, and Munchkinland.

Although the later *Oz* books were quietly allowed to go out-of-print in the 1970s, Baum's fourteen titles and many of his other fantasies were reissued again and again. His far-reaching appeal was particularly evidenced by the nonstop promulgation of foreign language editions of the *Oz* stories; by 1976, there had even been five original *Oz* books written in Russian by Alexandr Volkov. (Volkov first adapted *The Wizard of Oz* into Russian in 1939 and at that time — though cursorily acknowledging Baum — took primary credit for the narrative himself.)

Dedicated as ever, the thriving International Wizard of Oz Club championed an English translation of Volkov's first sequel in 1969 and really hit their stride by publishing two final manuscripts by Ruth Plumly Thompson: *Yankee in Oz* (1972) and *The Enchanted*

Preceding pages: Mego dolls patterned after MGM film characters pose before the Witch's Castle, one of three Oz playsets the company created for children in 1975-1976.

Right and above: Singer spent $2 million to promote its 1970 sponsorship of the annual *Oz* telecast and sold a repackaged edition of the soundtrack album as well.

Island of Oz (1976). In 1971, they also began printing a magazine of members' fiction, assembled and issued annually as *Oziana*.

Not surprisingly, there were by this time a number of impresarios who originated Oz entertainments in hopes of matching the success of MGM's film. (Not surprisingly, most of them failed.) Cinetron's *The Wonderful Land of Oz* — seen only in brief matinee appearances in 1969-1970 — was the first of several washouts. Produced and directed by Barry Mahon, the film was adapted from the second Oz book and damned by disinterest from children coast-to-coast; it quickly disappeared.

A similar fate befell a more ambitious project several years later. Producer Norman Prescott had recorded the songs and dialogue for a feature-length *Return to the Land of Oz* cartoon in 1962, and its potential seemed better than promising. The score was written by Sammy Cahn and James Van Heusen, and the cast of star voices included Ethel Merman, Danny Thomas, Milton Berle, Rise Stevens, and Margaret Hamilton. Prescott's real coup came when he signed sixteen-year-old Liza Minnelli for the role of Dorothy. Unfortunately, with only eleven minutes of finished footage, he ran out of money; it took ten years to complete the animation. The retitled *Journey Back to Oz* came and went at theaters in the United Kingdom in 1972, in the United States in 1974, and was soon thereafter relegated to afternoon television.

There was, however, life after MGM, and it took a pop/rock score, an awe-inspiring production, and a vibrant African-American cast to prove it. *The Wiz* came to Broadway in January 1975 with little advance publicity and no advance sale; the producers posted a provisional closing notice on opening night. But elated word-of-mouth and a quickly (but brilliantly) produced TV

Above: One-sheet poster for the weekend reissue appearances of MGM's *Oz* in 1970-1971.

We're off to the wonderful land of OZ! where scarecrows dance, and pumpkinheads sing, where wogglebugs talk and witches cast spells, where an enchanted little boy can live the magical adventures of his dreams.

CINETRON CORP
Presents

"THE WONDERFUL LAND OF OZ!"
so many thrills you'll be OZIFIED!

Produced and Directed by BARRY MAHON

Based on the L. FRANK BAUM Story

ALL NEW! ALL LIVE!
Never before shown anywhere!

CLASSIC/a DIVISION OF CINECOM CORP

Presented in glowing, glorious...
STORYBOOK COLOR

MATINEES ONLY! SATURDAY and SUNDAY!

commercial overcame both the show's somewhat shallow approach to the emotions of the story and the mixed critical notices. In the words of its hit song, *The Wiz* induced audiences to "ease on down the road" for four years and 1,672 exhilarating performances. Unfortunately, the contemporary tone of its humor and a misbegotten 1978 film adaptation dimmed any prospects of longevity for the property. But in its original Broadway incarnation, *The Wiz* was not only glorious fun but further demonstration of the everyman-adaptability and truth of Baum's original narrative.

Above: Pressbook cover for the matinee feature, *The Wonderful Land of Oz* (1969-1970). *Right:* Promotional cel for *Journey Back to Oz* (1974), the cartoon movie in which Mombi the Witch conquered the Emerald City with a herd of green elephants. The film was in production from 1962-1972; character voices were supplied by Mickey Rooney, Paul Lynde, Herschel Bernardi, Jack E. Leonard, and Paul Ford.

THE MOVIE!
Coming This Fall From Universal Pictures!

PREMIERE

**A Filmex Society Benefit for
The Los Angeles International Film Exposition**

Wednesday, October 25, 1978, 7:30 pm
Plitt's Century Plaza Theatre
ABC Entertainment Center
Century City
ADMIT ONE $10.00

Section	Row	Seat
RIGHT	GG	4

THE WIZ

The new musical version of "The Wonderful Wizard of Oz"

Souvenir program, above right, for Broadway's
The Wiz (1975). *Above:* Teaser poster for the
1978 film version. *Right:* Ticket to the movie
premiere; the ad art had changed considerably in the
intervening months, but nothing could save the $30
million flop. *Far right:* The Manhattan Transit
Authority promoted the New York subway system with
this 1978 poster. Dorothy and the Cowardly Lion from
The Wiz are shown in company with (among others)
Melba Moore, Eartha Kitt, Betsy Palmer, Martin
Balsam, Carol Channing, and cast members from
The Magic Show, Grease, Annie, and *Beatlemania.*

130

RE WAY TO MAKE IT TO BROADWAY

Subway

42nd St./8th Ave.

42nd St./Times Square

49th St./7th Ave.

50th St./8th Ave.

50th St./Broadway

7th Ave./53rd St.

Bus M6, M7 M10, M27 M104, M106

MTA gets you there

With the increased proliferation of products in the 1970s, it was easy for entire rooms to be done over in Oz decor. *Below:* Even Christmas trees could be Oz-themed after Kurt S. Adler, Inc. began marketing the first of its series of Ozzy holiday ornaments. *Above:* "Pop art" wood composition statues, posed on contemporary Oz fabric. *Right:* Metal Oz sculptures from Just Bernard.

RETURN

TO

OZ

1950s

REVISTA DE CROMOS

All roads led to the Emerald City in the 1980s; an Ozian omnipresence saturated the decade. Baby boomers who had grown to love the story on television or in the public domain book-push twenty years earlier were now presenting it to their own families — or their consumers. Astoundingly to some, happily to all, its cross-generational appeal never faltered, whether proffered as an at-home pleasure, a theatrical adventure, or a shopping opportunity. The personalities of Baum's magic world kept pace with every developing trend in presentation.

There was, by this time, more quantity than quality in much of the output. Home video only added to the prospects for film and television productions, but most of the contemporary efforts had as little prospect for longevity as their immediate predecessors. In the growing category of "more curious than classic": an animated *Thanksgiving in the Land of Oz* (1980; an original thirty-minute TV special with Sid Caesar as the voice of the Wizard), *The Wizard of Oz* (1983; a Japanese feature,

redubbed for American audiences with Lorne Greene as the voice of the Wizard), and *Dorothy Meets Ozma of Oz* (1988; a thirty-minute retelling of the third *Oz* book — without the Wizard). Rankin/Bass did a fine "animagic" adaptation of Baum's *The Life and Adventures of Santa Claus* for CBS-TV (1985), although their somewhat somber treatment precluded its revival as an annual holiday event. In 1988, Jim Henson went as far back as *Mother Goose In Prose* when announcing a string of his own Baum-inspired children's programs.

The most ambitious series of video presentations to date arrived in 1986 when Canada's Cinar Films introduced four feature-length cartoons — *The Wonderful Wizard of Oz, The Marvelous Land of Oz, Ozma of Oz,* and *The Emerald City of Oz* — assembled from fifty-two half-hour *Oz* adventures. (The latter were offered separately in their entirety as television programming.) Neither narration by Margot Kidder nor the major investment in storytelling time could overcome the dreary animation and Cinar's curious propensity for unnecessarily rewriting Baum's plots and devices.

The real *Oz* continued to find its outlet in bookstores, especially when Del Rey made available mass-market paperbacks of the fourteen Baum titles and (briefly) reprinted fifteen of the nineteen Thompson books as well. By this time, there were also countless original *Oz* stories written and (for the most part) privately printed by fans themselves. An outstanding contrast to the amateur efforts appeared in Eric Shanower's five "graphic novels," written and drawn for First Comics, and in two more *Oz* Club publications: *The Forbidden Fountain of Oz* (1980), by Eloise Jarvis McGraw and Lauren Lynn McGraw, and *The Ozmapolitan of Oz* (1986) by Dick Martin.

Preceding pages: Disney's *Return to Oz* (1985) inspired international merchandising. The Dorothy doll was crafted by Zapf Puppen in Germany; her companions came from Heart & Heart in Japan.

Above: This Spanish sticker book retold the *Oz* story with scenes from the 1986 Cinar cartoon series.

In the decade's most important enterprise, the Disney Studios launched themselves into Ozian territory after thirty years of aspiration. (They'd held film rights to a dozen Baum Oz titles since 1956, originally intending to star TV's "Mouseketeers" in a 1957 musical, *Rainbow Road to Oz*.) In 1985, Disney produced a much-heralded, $27-million live-action *Return to Oz*; the results were bittersweet. Extremely well-cast, the picture offered visually breathtaking representations of the Baum/Neill concepts of Oz, including first-rate character re-creations, expert "Claymation" incarnations of the gnomes, and the indelible image of the Gump as it flew across the moon. Unfortunately, a dark and almost humorless script sank the film as joyless, emotionally uninvolving entertainment for a mass audience. Though more successful abroad than in the United States, *Return to Oz* was a mystery in its heavy-handed approach to a lighthearted land.

Part of its demise could be traced to the ongoing ardor felt by so many for the MGM film, which remained a public delight. Even a 1980 home video release didn't preclude another decade of ratings triumph for the Garland picture as an annual television event.

Right: Toy PVC figures from Spain, modeled after the Cinar cartoons (1988).

The magic diversified as well. In 1987, London's Royal Shakespeare Company premiered a stage presentation that for the first time utilized both the film score and screenplay. Its reception led to a less-successful arena tour in the United States in 1989, emblazoned by special effects but sunk by an entirely prerecorded acting/singing soundtrack for the "live" cast. Original movie memorabilia continued to command headline-making prices at auction, culminating in a $165,000 bid for a pair of ruby slippers in 1988. And even MGM was astounded at the outpouring of emotion and media attention generated by the film's fiftieth anniversary. At the height of the 1989 hoopla, the Library of Congress and National Film Registry announced that *The Wizard of Oz* was one of the first twenty-five motion pictures to be designated a "National Treasure."

Above: The Downey rebate certificate from the fiftieth anniversary video was so beautifully designed that most people didn't redeem it (1989).

137

Αν υπάρχει κάτι που σίγουρα πρέπει να δείτε, αυτό είναι...

ο**Μαγικός Κόσμος** του **Οz**

★ RETURN TO OZ ★

Η WALT DISNEY παρουσιάζει ένα θαύμα αριστουργηματικής φαντασίας, σε μια ταινία που θα γοητεύσει!

Πρωταγωνιστούν:

ΝΙΚΟΛ ΟΥΤΛΙΑΜΣΟΝ · ΤΖΗΝ ΜΑΡΣ · ΠΑΤΠΕΡ ΛΩΡΗ και η αξιαγάπητη ΦΑΤΡΟΥΖΑ ΜΠΑΛΚ

Σκηνοθεσία: ΓΟΥΩΛΤΕΡ ΜΑΡΤΣ   Μουσική: ΝΤΕΗΒΙΝΤ ΣΑΪΡ

WALT DISNEY PRODUCTION · ΕΓΧΡΩΜΟ · CINEMA INTERNATIONAL CORPORATION

R*eturn to Oz* concept art, below, by Michael Ploog for the design of the Scarecrow. *Above:* The Greek film poster. *Left:* A British picture puzzle. *Far left (clockwise from top):* Australian standee display, Japanese theater program, German comic book, Japanese Heart & Heart toy figurines, and British drinking mugs (a premium from Total Motor Oil).

SCARECROW

PLOOG

The Scarecrow, a Wheeler, Tik-Tok, and Jack Pumpkinhead as baked-clay maquettes — the first three-dimensional stage of preparation for their *Return to Oz* characterizations. *Left and below:* French posters tout the "ExtraOZdinaire" film personalities; ten-year-old Fairuza Balk made a charming and sincere Dorothy but couldn't save the dour scenario. *Far right:* "Keep On Dreamin'" was a new song added as underscoring to the film end credits in Japan and released as a single record there.

WALT DISNEY PICTURES présente

OZ

un Monde Extraordinaire

EXTRA OZ DINAIRE DOROTHY!

SORTIE LE 23 OCTOBRE

WALT DISNEY PICTURES présente

OZ

un Monde Extraordinaire

EXTRA OZ DINAIRE ÉPOUVANTAIL!

... having said one last good-bye, she clapped the heels of her shoes together three times, saying, "Take me home to Aunt Em!"

Left: The top right Tik-Tok figurine was an instant scarcity, created solely as a souvenir for those who attended the film's British premiere. The Royal Army of Oz medallion (center) was another promotional keepsake, as were all three Oz keys — the latter provided as mementos for the movie crew. The remaining items, molded plastic character pins, were sold at Tokyo Disneyland.

ディズニー映画
「オズ」イメージ・ソング

KEEP ON DREAMIN'

歌 タケカワユキヒデ

Return To
OZ
オズ

CH-127-DR
Disneyland
RECORD
STEREO
¥700

© MCMLXXXV WALT DISNEY PRODUCTIONS

CH-127
T4988 001 02091 2   H2-21

SIDE 2

KEEP ON
DREAMIN'
(インストゥルメント)

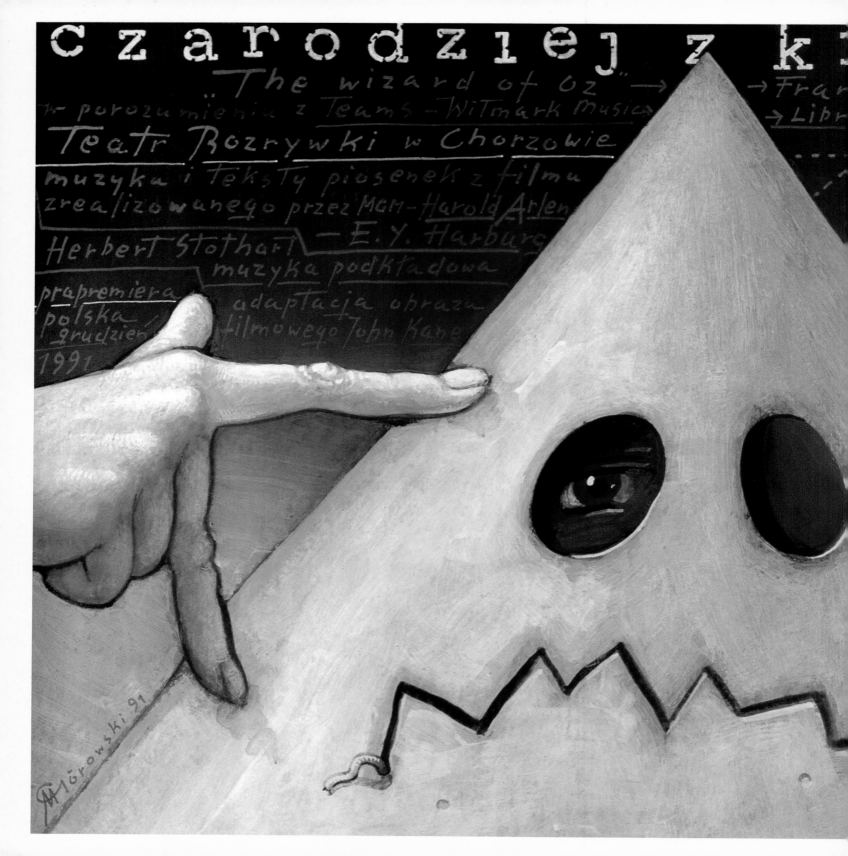

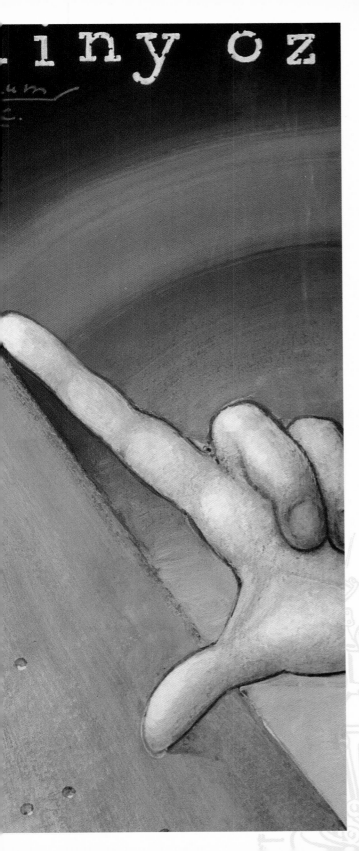

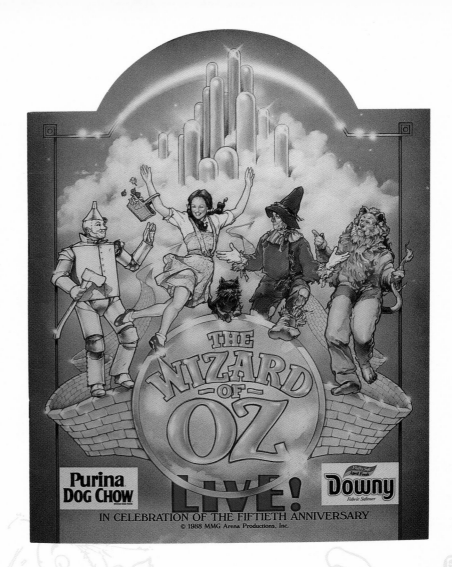

Worldwide stage versions of *The Wizard of Oz* first began to multiply in the 1960s and culminated with the debut of the Royal Shakespeare adaptation of the MGM film in 1987. *Left: The Wizard* appears in Poland (1991). *Above: The Wizard of Oz Live!* was an ambitious, arena-scaled variation of the movie, but its lackluster prerecorded dialogue, songs, and music disappointed audiences; much of the show's scheduled tour was canceled (1989).

The Scarecrow was now ruler of the Emerald City, and although he was not a Wizard, the people were proud of him. "For," they said, "there is not another city in all the world that is ruled by a stuffed man." And, so far as they knew, they were quite right.

Macy's celebrated the MGM film's fiftieth anniversary by sponsoring three weeks of in-house Oz events; their Herald Square store was decorated throughout with Oz statues, flags, clocks, and carpeting (1989). *Right:* These fiftieth-anniversary music boxes were available only in Japan. *Far right (clockwise from bottom right):* Oz Music Boxes — Dorothy and Glinda (1981) and Dorothy in the Haunted Forest (1983) from Seymour Mann; book-inspired characters, made in Japan (circa early 1970s); Dorothy and the Scarecrow (circa 1970s); Dorothy and the Tin Woodman from Schmid (1983); Dorothy and Toto from Spencer Gifts (1974); the Tin Woodman from Seymour Mann (1981); the Scarecrow and Lion from Schmid (1983; center rear); the Lion, Dorothy, and the Scarecrow from Seymour Mann (1981).

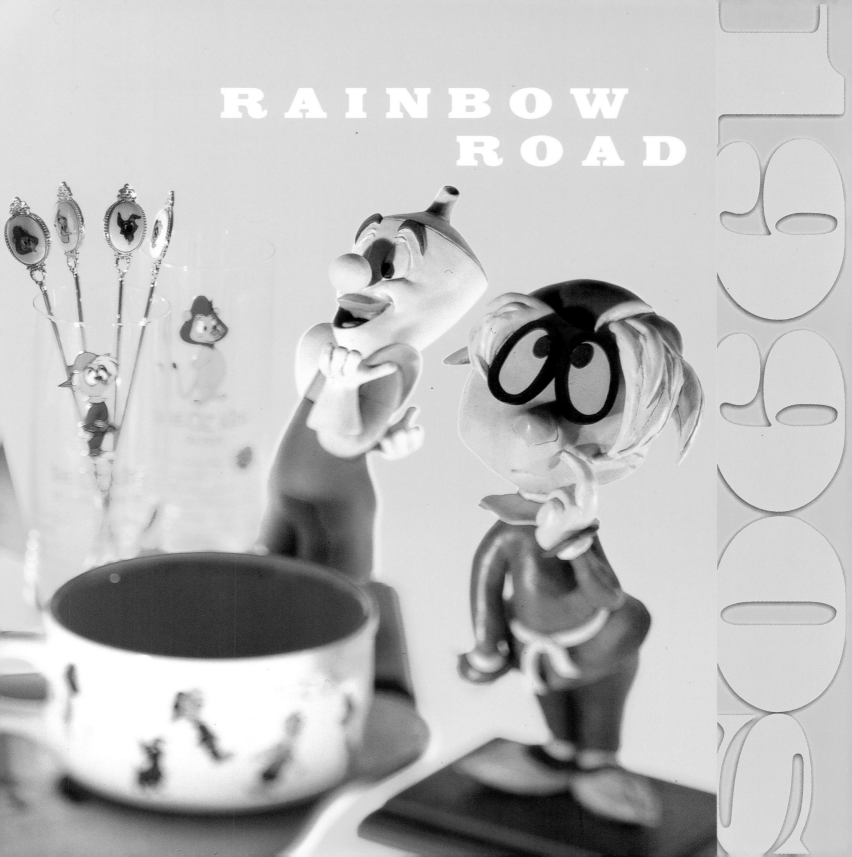

When other twentieth-century icons hit their special anniversaries, they savored a flurry of excitement and merchandising . . . followed by the public's swift segue to the next celebration. *The Wizard of Oz* proved a singular exception to tradition; after (or because of) the 1989 tumult, both the MGM film and Baum's world only gained in momentum as esteemed and (sometimes even nicely) exploited properties.

The legend and licensing of MGM's *Oz* never stopped. Already a 1980s best-seller, the film videotape soared to cumulative sales of six million units by 1998. At Orlando's Disney/MGM Studios Theme Park, the climax of their Great Movie Ride came in its saunter through Oz. The United States Postal Service put Judy Garland and Toto on a 1990 stamp in commemoration of major films of 1939. The same year also brought a Saturday morning network cartoon series, utilizing the movie characterizations and sound-alike voices.

When the Las Vegas MGM Grand Hotel opened in 1993, an Oz motif was everywhere apparent in its decor and attractions. Adaptations of the film continued to appear as "live" events: a benefit *The Wizard of Oz In Concert*, televised from New York's Lincoln Center (1995); a touring (and television special) *The Wizard of Oz On Ice* (which debuted in 1995); and both full-length and condensed versions of the Royal Shakespeare script, which played virtually everywhere.

Preceding pages: Merchandise from The Oz Kids Store, Tokyo's exclusive marketplace for products inspired by the animated TV series (1995). The "Tin Boy" and "Scarecrow, Jr." figures on the right are one-of-a-kind non-commercial maquettes, created at Hyperion Entertainment as preliminary models for the two cartoon characters.

There were welcome variations from the MGMania. NBC offered a glowing TV movie, *The Dreamer of Oz*, for Christmas 1990 and, despite slightly rewritten history and a few slow sequences, the Baum biographical drama was a stylish, warmly performed endeavor. Earlier that year, the Hollywood Goldwyn Library mounted a Baum exhibition — one of many assembled on behalf of Oz and/or its creators all over the country by the 1990s. Paul Taylor's *Oz*, an original ballet based on Baum characters, premiered at New York's City Center in 1992. In 1993, the Oz Club added another "official" book to the series by publishing *The Wicked Witch of Oz* by Rachel Cosgrove Payes, designed and illustrated in best tradition by Eric Shanower.

The decade also brought an inspired approach to Oz animation when Hyperion Entertainment produced twenty-six episodes of *The Oz Kids* (1995). The innovative concept followed the adventures of the offspring of the famous Baum characters; so popular were the programs in Japan that an "Oz Kids" Store was established there. Individual shows were later combined

Above: Soundtrack compact disc for the animated Asian TV series, "The Space Adventure of Oz."

into eight feature-length videos for sale in the United States.

Garnering additional attention in the 1990s were the well-established "Oz Festivals" that first sprang up during the preceding decade. Anywhere from ten- to sixty-thousand people annually attended weekend events in Chittenango, New York (Baum's birthplace), Grand Rapids, Minnesota (Garland's birthplace), and — especially — Chesterton, Indiana, where a gift shop and museum had evolved into a virtual "Oz Central" for Midwesterners. The major attraction at each gathering was the appearance "in person" of surviving Munchkin actors from the MGM film. (In Liberal, Kansas, a vintage farm dwelling was reconfigured as "Dorothy's House," drawing year-round tourists.)

Finally, to the accompaniment of affectionate audience and media farewells, the network television contracts for MGM's *Oz* finally lapsed in 1998 after the film's thirty-ninth telecast in forty-two years. (The property was assured a future home on cable.) To herald its upcoming sixtieth anniversary, *The Wizard of Oz* was also booked into 1,800 theaters in autumn 1998, quickly adding $14 million to its box office gross. As the millennium approached, there were plans for further MGM-inspired events, a Baum/MGM Kansas theme park, and a centennial Oz book.

Reading fell far behind television and video as home entertainment for children during the second half of the century. Yet even without the necessity or encouragement of old, a happy percentage of young readers continued to annually acquire and read tens of thousands of Oz titles; today's bookstores offer hardcover facsimiles or inexpensive paperbacks of much of the series. Baum's serendipitous creation has endured not as dusty history but as a "real, truly live place" — an alternate universe that thrives and pulses with laughter and love, both imbued by the passions of its fans.

The unique position of Oz in American literature and culture can perhaps be most clearly acknowledged by the fact that it is now virtually impossible to find a man or woman or child over the age of two who can't immediately identify a picture of Dorothy and her friends. And with each recognition comes a rush of joy, excitement, memory. One hundred years of Oz has quite simply meant one hundred years of unparalleled, incomparable magic.

Above: Souvenirs and promotional material from the Oz-oriented era of the Las Vegas MGM Grand Hotel (1993-1996).

149

Mounted together on an *Ozzy* base, each Silvestri snow globe depicted a different highlight of Dorothy's adventure (1995).

"Where is Kansas?" asked the man, in surprise. "I don't know," replied Dorothy, sorrowfully; "but it is my home, and I'm sure it's somewhere."

An animation cel and matching background, above, from the Saturday morning TV series based on MGM's *The Wizard of Oz* (1990–1991). *Right:* The United States Postal Service celebrated four classic 1939 movies with this block of first-class stamps (1990). *Below:* Between 1980 and 1998, the MGM film received multiple repackagings for the home video market.

THE DREAMER OF OZ

BEDROCK
Adam
PRODUCTIONS

NBC

On the NBC Television Network.

A New Movie Premiering in December

MILLENNIUM
1 DEC
$3.95 US
$5.25 CAN

OzSQUAD

THE ORIGINAL
OZ SERIES!

Promotional poster, left, for the TV movie, *The Dreamer of Oz,* in which John Ritter forsook his usual comedic turns to effectively portray L. Frank Baum (1990). *Above:* First issues of *Oz Squad* and *Oz,* alternative "dark side" graphic novels (1995). *Right:* Creature Features produced this collectible, sculpted-resin model of an horrific winged monkey in 1996.

The *Wizard of Oz On Ice*, far left, featured a prerecorded soundtrack on which all character voices except Dorothy were performed by comic Bobby McFerrin (1995). *Above left:* Souvenir program for the ninety-minute stage version of the MGM film that played New York's Madison Square Garden in 1997 prior to an extensive tour. The initial engagement featured TV's Roseanne as Miss Gulch/The Wicked Witch of the West. *Left:* This 1992 German production had an original script but used the MGM score. *Above right:* The 1994 Israeli *Wizard* had new songs except for "Over the Rainbow." *Right:* There was even a Dorothy/Barbie modelled on Michal Yannai, the popular Israeli singer who starred in the show.

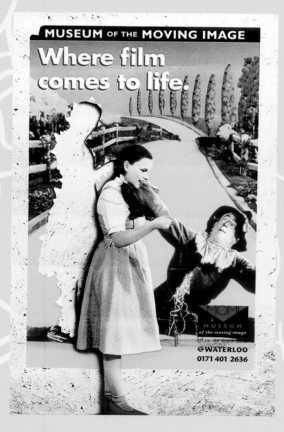

Poster, below, for the Museum of the Moving Image at the British Film Institute in London.
Left: Cover art for The Oz Kids video, *The Return of Mombi* (1996).
Right: A century of Oz comes full circle: 1990s Oz Kids character pins perch atop the open pages of a 1900 first edition of *The Wonderful Wizard of Oz.*

Acknowledgments

Kacy Andrews, Woolsey Ackerman, Patty Fricke, Todd Gajdusek, Jon Jankowsky, Marc Lewis, Tod Robert Machin, Fred M. Meyer, Brent Phillips, Ryan Sucher, Lena Tabori, Elaine Willingham, Tom Wilhite...And fellow travelers no longer with us: Dorothy and Jim Nitch, Frederick E. Otto, and Rob Roy MacVeigh.

Photography Credits

Pages 1, 68 (left), 70 (top left), 72-73 (background image), 75 (Black and white photo inset), 80 (bottom), and 96 are Copyright © 1999 by Warner Bros. Courtesy of Warner Bros. Publishing. All Rights Reserved.

Page 130: "The Wiz" poster is Copyright © 1999 by Universal City Studios, Inc. Courtesy of Universal Studios Publishing Rights. All Rights Reserved.

Page 140: Two posters from "Return to Oz" are Copyright © 1999 by The Walt Disney Company. Courtesy of Disney Publishing Group. All Rights Reserved.

Photographer's credits:

Mark Hill: 5, 6-7, 18, 20-21, 38-39, 50 (bottom right), 53, 55, 56, 57, 58 (background), 60-61, 66 (top left), 67, 71, 72 (inset), 74, 77, 78-79, 80, 81 (top right), 94-95, 101, 104-105, 112-113, 116-117 (background), 118, 119, 120, 122-123, 124-125, 132 (top left) 132-133 (background), 134-135, 138, 145, 146-147, 150-151 (background), 153 (background), and 157.

All other photographs: Richard Glenn.

Also...

For further information on all things Baum and Oz, please send a self-addressed, stamped, business envelope to:
The International Wizard of Oz Club, Inc.
P. O. Box 266
Kalamazoo, MI 49004-0266.

Left: Detail from the center-spread illustration in the 1949 MGM record of songs from *The Wizard of Oz. Following page:* The last chapter of *The Wonderful Wizard of Oz.*

Home Again

AUNT EM had just come out of the house to water the cabbages when she looked up and saw Dorothy running toward her.

"My darling child!" she cried, folding the little girl in her arms and covering her face with kisses; "where in the world did you come from?"

"From the land of Oz," said Dorothy, gravely. "And here is Toto, too. And oh, Aunt Em! I'm so glad to be at home again!"

THE END